TWENTY CONTROVERSIAL ISSUES IN CHRISTENDOM

In Essentials, Unity;
In Non-Essentials, Liberty;
In All Things, Charity

TWENTY CONTROVERSIAL ISSUES IN CHRISTENDOM

From an Editorial Columnist's Point of View

Stephen Rowland

CrossBooks™
A Division of LifeWay
1663 Liberty Drive
Bloomington, IN 47403
www.crossbooks.com
Phone: 1-866-879-0502

© 2012 Stephen Rowland. All rights reserved.

No part of this book may be reproduced, stored in a retrieval system, or transmitted by any means without the written permission of the author.

First published by CrossBooks: 8/17/2012

ISBN: 978-1-4627-2046-0 (sc)
ISBN: 978-1-4627-2048-4 (hc)
ISBN: 978-1-4627-2047-7 (e)

Library of Congress Control Number: 2012914290

Printed in the United States of America

This book is printed on acid-free paper.

Any people depicted in stock imagery provided by Thinkstock are models, and such images are being used for illustrative purposes only.

Certain stock imagery © Thinkstock.

Because of the dynamic nature of the Internet, any web addresses or links contained in this book may have changed since publication and may no longer be valid. The views expressed in this work are solely those of the author and do not necessarily reflect the views of the publisher, and the publisher hereby disclaims any responsibility for them.

Contents

Preface	ix
Acknowledgments	xi
1. Do Good Christians Avoid Controversy?	1
2. Politics and Christianity	5
Christians Shouldn't Get Involved in Politics…	6
Progressive Secularism	9
Is it Illegal to Teach the Bible in Public Schools?	12
Neither Theocracy nor Democracy	15
3. Islam and Christianity	19
Busting the Myth of Poverty-Bred Terrorists	20
Flushing the Quran	23
The Crusades – Whose Fault?	26
A Christian Fundamentalist Jihad	29
Tolerance Doesn't Require Submission	32
Peace-Loving versus Abrogation and Taqiyya	35
4. Science and the Bible	39
Science and Christian Belief — Incompatible?	40
Scientific Measurement of Religious Experience	43
Psychological Experimentation and Human Nature	46
Did Galileo Discredit the Christian Conception of our Solar System?	49
Does Prayer Help in Mathematics?	52

Einstein's Theory of Relativity and Religious Relativism	55
Improbability of Life Evolving from Green Slime	58
Evolution is Evolving	61
The Skeleton in the Closet of Creationism	64
The Middle Ground	67
Gerald Schroeder's Time Relativity Solution	70
Suppressing Intelligent Design	73
Earth — Tailor Made for Homo Sapiens	76

5. Racism and Christianity   79

Racism in the Church	80
Interracial Marriage	83
Martin Luther King Jr. and Christian Social Action	86
Does the Bible Condone Slavery?	89
Christians Drove Abolition	92
"Christian" Identity Movement	95

6. Pacifism and Gun Rights   99

Was Jesus a Pacifist?	100
The Middle Ground Between Pacifism and Militarism	104
Handgun Permits – Not for Christians?	108
"Christian" Militias?	111

7. Homosexuality and Christianity   115

Obama's Gay Rights Theology	116
Genetics is the Key?	119
Jesus Never Said Anything About It …	124
Gay Agenda Chips Away at Freedom	127
Should You Have a Gay Friend?	130

8.	**Abortion and Christianity**	**133**
	Stalwart Sweeties vs. Wanton Wenches	134
	Do the Unborn Feel Pain?	137
	The Big Bang and Abortion	140
	Genetic Defects and Abortion	143
9.	**Prosperity Theology**	**147**
	Scam Artists Part I	148
	Scam Artists Part II	151
	Hard Times for Prosperity Preachers	154
	Job Promotion and Prosperity	157
	Rewarding Activities Seldom Bring Wealth	160
	No Such Thing as a Christian Beggar?	163
	What is a Successful Christian Life?	166
	Are Prayers for National Prosperity Misguided?	169
10.	**Biblical Interpretation**	**173**
	Red Letter Christians	174
	Automatic Writing?	177
	Implications of the Dead Sea Scrolls	180
	The Gnostics versus Scriptural Authority	183
	KJV Only?	186
11.	**Interdenominational Cooperation – Impossible?**	**189**
	The Value of Differing Denominations	190
	A Cooperative Model	193
	Compassion is Not Political	197
	Striving for Christian Unity	199
	Disagreeing Agreeably	202
	Book of Galatians – Pursue Unity	206
	Judgment Calls – "Blessing of the Animals"	209

12. Social Drinking – OK?	**213**
Teetotalers versus Social Drinkers	214
Alcoholism and Genetics	217
13. Illegal Immigration	**221**
Illegal Immigration Issue	222
Border Control	225
14. Divine Healing: When Bad Theology Becomes Real Tragedy	**229**
15. Marriage and Christianity	**233**
Marriage – a Dying Institution?	234
Why are Christian Marriages Failing?	237
16. Does Spanking Promote Violence?	**241**
17. Prostitution — the "Victimless Crime"?	**245**
18. World Overpopulation – Menace or Myth?	**249**
19. The Decline of America?	**253**
The Tip of the Iceberg	254
The Generational Slippery Slope	257
It's No Myth	260
20. The Bible is Simple so Why Seminaries?	**263**
Intellectual Curiosity	264
Pursuing that Master's Degree	267
Advanced Biblical Studies Foster Humility	270
Holier Than Thou? Not a Bible Scholar…	273
Footnotes	277
About the Author	281

Preface

I am not a person who enjoys controversy. My personality is more introverted than extroverted; I enjoy working together in harmony much more than poking and prodding for areas of disagreement. When political discussions "turn up the heat" at family gatherings, I am inclined to provide conciliatory remarks or even attempt to change the course of discussion. There is a bit of truth to that old maxim of avoiding politics and religion at the dinner table. It might seem odd that my first book presents twenty areas of controversy relevant to Christianity.

Perhaps my reticence for controversy stems in part from our culture that seemingly grows more crude and uncivil through the passing decades. We seem to be losing the art of disagreeing agreeably. That noticeable trend (especially in politics) can filter into matters of Christian thought and discussion providing a damaging "testimony" to non-believers when they observe Christians skewering each other over doctrinal differences. That is certainly not the intent of this book.

I fully expect genuine, intelligent, and spiritually mature Christian readers to disagree with two or three (or more!) of my opinions in this book — that in no manner casts a suspicious light on their devotion to Christ. I sometimes find that I disagree with myself on certain issues as the years go by! I think the motto of the Restorationist movement is apropos here: "In Essentials, Unity; in Non-essentials, Liberty; in All Things, Charity."

The dangers in habitually avoiding anything of a controversial nature as a Christian outweigh the unintentional slights that others might feel due to the discussions. American culture is increasingly moving to a post-Christian stance in many areas which accentuates areas of controversy between a Christian and secular worldview. If we never take the time to seriously examine the issues in-depth, Christians will increasingly be viewed as beholden to an antiquated and logically indefensible worldview. Our children are often unprepared for the culture shock and sometimes outright ridicule they will be exposed to if they choose to attend a secular university. Sequestering ourselves behind our church walls only insures the increasing alienation of future generations of our children from academia and the culture at large. The Apostle Peter's stance on dialoguing with those outside the Christian faith can be found in 1 Peter 3:15, "Always be prepared to give an answer to everyone who asks you to give the reason for the hope that you have" (NIV). That is the spirit in which I have written these articles for *The Daily Herald* that were source material for this book.

A few of these articles deal more with in-church issues of theology more than countenancing a secular worldview. The value of these is the potential to discover presuppositions of which we were unaware, whether personal or denominational. There is great value in understanding the scriptural view of someone outside your circle of friends and denominational affiliation even if you don't agree with the view. You will have a better understanding of the person, their hermeneutical method, and every once in a while find a new valuable insight you couldn't have discovered any other way. May God bless you richly in the search for His truth.

Acknowledgments

First I should mention my mother who departed this life on December 7, 2004 to be with her Lord. She bought my first study Bible when I was a teenager with a handwritten note inside the front cover quoting 2 Timothy 2:15: "Study to shew thyself approved unto God, a workman that needeth not to be ashamed, rightly dividing the word of truth" (KJV). Secondly I should mention a succession of Godly pastors throughout my life, all of whom drove home the concept that a genuine saving relationship with Jesus Christ affects every area of your life throughout the week — not simply what we do on Sunday morning. One particular minister recently stands out in this regard — Russ Adcox of Maury Hills Church in Columbia, TN. Not long ago he preached a series of messages on "Questions Christians Hate" that I thought to be a courageous move on the part of a minister of the gospel; many churches consciously avoid those topics despite being extremely relevant to our modern society. That series was part of the inspiration for this book. Thirdly I must give credit to my mentors at Global University who prodded me into examining Biblical issues from a variety of authors' views during my pursuit of a master's degree in Biblical Literature. Understanding different hermeneutical models and utilizing the "REV" principle (reflection, evaluation, and valuation) will serve me well in future endeavors. Fourthly, I would like to thank English Literature major Janet King for editing this book and saving me from many a grammatical embarrassment. She refused any monetary compensation whatsoever stating that she enjoyed every article and was simply grateful for being a part of the creation of this book; she was a big blessing. Finally, I would like to acknowledge the patience of my wife Susan and our three year old grandson Brendan during those long stretches of time that I was secluded in my study den. It was during one of those study sessions that little Brendan appeared outside my doorway with a concerned air and a half smile inquiring, "Papa, do you need help?"

DO GOOD CHRISTIANS AVOID CONTROVERSY?

Over the past eight years I've written quite a few "feel good" editorials such as the ones about Project Compassion, Charity Biker Runs, People Helping People, and showing God's love by helping the poor. I've also written about controversial topics in the Christian world such as conservatives vs. liberals, religion in politics and vice versa, homosexuality, abortion, intelligent design vs. evolutionism, racism in churches, labor unions, socialism vs. capitalism, pacifistic Christians vs. handgun carry permits, Biblical slavery, Israel vs. Palestinians, the "King James Only" issue, prosperity preachers, and much more. I have had some folks question the propriety of a Christian writing strong editorials on such controversial issues, knowing that some readers will be offended by my views. I have no doubt that even some pastors (or ministers) have been occasionally irked by a particular view I espoused. The objection that I've heard goes something like this – "Christians should be promoting unity and love at all times and should never be arguing or offending other Christian brothers and sisters. To do so knowingly and regularly is the sin of being divisive – bringing strife into the Body of Christ."

Why do I write certain editorials about controversial topics? Well, first of all, that's what an editorial columnist does. Facts, statistics, logic, analysis, moralizing, persuasive appeals — it is all part of what readers expect on the editorial page. If they are easily offended then they can skip the editorial page. If an editorialist only wrote about non-controversial subjects without much "heart" using poorly researched and weakly supported opinions, then people would eventually stop reading his articles – and justifiably so.

But it goes much further than the mere job description. If Christians purposely shy away from expressing themselves on newsworthy controversial topics, then the "vacuum" created thereby will result in people generally thinking that Christianity is largely irrelevant to the important issues of the day. Christians would be perceived as being ill-informed, somewhat dull in mental faculties, or stuck in an outdated worldview. The implication will be — go to church to make yourself a more moral person, but if you want to help solve important societal problems, then leave your Christianity behind. That's precisely what many Christian young people do when they go off to attend universities – they leave their Christianity behind.

So what does it mean to be a divisive person who promotes needless strife? Arguing about the color of the church carpet (non-essentials); crusading for converts in your church to your view on minor doctrinal points (schisms, factions); belittling the pastor/minister in an effort to discredit him in front of others (rebellion, character assassination); manipulating things behind the scenes in order to get your way (church politics); arguing about who is the best preacher or leader (jealousy, envy) — if you are in the habit of doing these sort of things then shame on you – you are a divisive person. If, however, you are courteously discussing current Biblical or societal issues which may be controversial then that is not only acceptable for Christians but actually beneficial. Differing views and interpretations need to be heard; sometimes that's the way erroneous concepts are revealed and discredited while fresh Biblical truths may be rediscovered.

There are some good ground rules to follow along this path – don't attack people or churches, rather discuss the issues specifically. Don't vent your venom; share the facts and your interpretation of them civilly. Also you might want to research your opponent's view well enough to argue his side if you were forced to do so. You may discover some points you hadn't considered; sometimes you might actually end up modifying your view. I've personally discovered I was wrong on a few issues. It's amazing to me how many folks put those blinders on – the party blinders in politics, or the denomination blinders in religious discussions – and never investigate opposing views because they know they are right to start with.

I don't lose much sleep with the few readers who are offended by my editorials. It's inevitable. They have the choice to skip the editorial page or even pick up a pen and write a letter to the editor explaining their view. Instead they want to tell me (or you) what you should or should not be writing about. Remember, if you are a Christian, then it is a mark of spiritual maturity not to be easily offended! (Proverbs 19:11).

POLITICS AND CHRISTIANITY

Christians Shouldn't Get Involved in Politics...

While growing up in a conservative household and attending an evangelical church, there were certain unwritten rules that everyone knew. One was that Christians were to be "separate from the world" — that we were to live our lives in devotion to Christ and not center our affections on popularity, the keeping up with the Jones materialistic mindset, pop culture with its entertainment idol worship, the party scene, etc.

"Pushing the envelope" would have meant helping out the church staff in mailings or offerings. Blending into the background with anonymous acts of service was much preferable to being a Christian Superstar on platform, stage, or in front of a TV camera. Too much popularity can feed so easily into the human ego with its never satiated lust for more — more public affirmation, more contributions to "my ministry," more church members, more church authority and power, more of my plans and positive feedback. Constructive criticism or perceptive course-altering advice from mature and trusted friends suddenly becomes viewed as vicious attacks motivated by Satan on "God's minister." Anything negative is put into the doubt category opposite of the faith category. Living in a bubble of only positive affirmation leads so easily to the dictator mindset, whether in politics or the ministry. That vicious cycle leading to highly embarrassing public scandals of church leaders (and politicians) has headlined quite a few news stories over the last few months.

Wanting to avoid treading the never-ending "more power" trail, most church members and ministers really wanted to avoid the limelight preferring to work in the background. There was also an unwritten "Rule No. 2" in effect — "Christians shouldn't get involved in politics." Politics and the lawyer profession were viewed in the same light — both professions were fraught with selfish corruption, and the more one involved himself with either, the more likely one was to succumb eventually to the morally corrupt milieu. Politicians, lawyers and used car salesmen were all lumped together in the untrustworthy category — one of those truly egalitarian classless categories where level of education or social standing were irrelevant. Running for public office was never construed to be a Christian calling.

Being separate from the world and avoiding politics over the decades eventually had its inevitable result — those of traditional Christian faith became seen as old-fashioned leftovers from a prior age who were never at the vanguard of any prominent social movement. Blending into the background eventually resulted in being viewed as anachronistic — strangely out of place and time. Liberalism prevailed in universities, Hollywood, and the editorial pages of newspapers.

Traditional Christians became "Fundamentalists" — unstable kooks with all the intellectual prowess of slugs. America would surely follow the path that Europe took: ever-increasing secularism to the point of churches and Cathedrals being abandoned and turned into tourist attractions. The gray-haired, never-yielding conservatives would gradually fade into the oblivion of natural causes, while their children would be educated into modern progressivism in public schools. You don't do paradigm change by convincing the zealots — you let them slowly die out and re-educate their children.

Obviously that paradigm-changing scheme hasn't exactly played itself out on cue over the last twenty years or so. Traditional conservatives started voting in record numbers from the Reagan years into the Bush years. Christian academies and home schooling became popular alternatives. I've never seen so many Democrats run on conservative social issues and reference God so much in their speeches. If they aren't genuine then they most assuredly deserve Oscars. They made some of the Republican candidates look left-of-center.

Hollywood recently has reevaluated its shunning of Christian traditional values, following the trail blazed by *The Passion of the Christ* with movies such as *The Chronicles of Narnia: The Lion, the Witch, and the Wardrobe* (inspired by Christian philosopher C.S. Lewis). Legions of Christians went to law school, and now we have organizations such as the Alliance Defense Fund representing religious liberty cases in court and winning most of them (a fact that is quite disconcerting to the ACLU).

NBC recently relented on its censored version of Veggie Tales after public outcry and will now release them with all references to God and scripture intact. Wal-Mart recently made concessions in its financial support of the gay-rights agenda in response to a proposed nationwide boycott.

It's too early to proclaim the death of Christian traditionalism in America — we decided to engage the world, get educated, and get politically involved. As long as we don't get infatuated with ourselves, there's still hope.

Progressive Secularism

Not long ago Rev. Daniel Coughlin (chaplain of the House) said a prayer for God's blessings on the 109th Congress in a prayer service attended by both Democrats and Republicans. During his presidency George W. Bush reiterated his support for abstinence-based programs and also promised that faith-based charitable organizations (such as The Salvation Army) would be eligible for Federal tax dollars in local or state social programs. It's news like that which drives progressive secularists into an emotional state of distraction: Michael Newdow (famous for challenging the "under God" phrase in the Pledge of Allegiance) filed suit to block public prayers at President Bush's inaugural ceremony. Apparently he felt the "separation of church and state" principle was being violated and feared that conservatives were gradually paving the way for a "theocracy." I think their fears were quite unjustified.

A "theocracy" is a form of government run by the religious elite. The litmus test for candidacy is to be an adherent of the particular religion, denomination, or sect that is officially approved and permanently incumbent - no others need apply. Civil laws are modeled on that sect's interpretation of religious law, and other religions are severely discriminated against or banned outright; an example would be Iran's "mullahacracy." Avoiding persecution by an officially established denomination (Church of England) is what drove the Pilgrims to America.

If there are religious conservatives advocating that type of government, I'm unaware of it. There is a proper balance, a healthy tension, that should be maintained between people of faith and secularists in the public arena. I personally would not want a public school teacher instructing my child on how to offer-up prayers to Allah, but neither would I want to see voluntary student-led prayers banned. Learning about various world religions is a legitimate part of social studies, while banning Christian symbols and greetings at Christmas and Easter is simply being intolerant. Government officials should not actively promote a particular faith or denomination as government policy, but neither should personal expressions of faith be censored on the public square. Jefferson's idea of "separation of church and state" (not mentioned in any of our nation's founding documents) was intended to prevent history from repeating itself- the Pilgrim's nightmare of a state-established denomination. The First Amendment was intended to promote freedom OF religion, not freedom FROM religion.

If that is not the correct interpretation, there would never have been such as "chaplain of the House," Presidential proclamations of a "Day of Prayer," references to the "Creator" and "Divine Providence" in the Declaration of Independence, and the fact that every session of Congress opens with an official prayer. Some people are absolutely stunned when they discover our nation's first public schools used textbooks like *The New England Primer* and *Webster's Blue-backed Speller* - both filled with Bible verses and moral stories. The very first system of public education on the North American Continent was established in 1647 by the Massachusetts School Law, and part of that law promoted the reading of the Bible in public schoolrooms.

Progressive secularists do the general public a real disservice by insinuating that their cause is supported by the deism espoused by a few of our nation's Founding Fathers. Examples: Patrick Henry and George Washington favored a proposal using federal tax money to support different denominations of Christian churches! Now some people are contemplating taxing churches - what a switch. Benjamin Franklin was the gentleman who implored the Constitutional Delegates to open every session of Congress with a prayer from a clergyman. Thomas Jefferson ended a National Prayer with the following quote: "In times of prosperity, fill our hearts with thanksgiving, and, in the day of trouble, suffer not our trust in Thee to fail; all of which we ask through Jesus Christ our Lord. Amen." Deists were favorably disposed to public expressions of Christian faith - progressive secularists simply do not have a legitimate historical/constitutional leg to stand on. That is why they avoid direct quotations and Constitutional framers' "original intent" like the Bubonic Plague, and argue instead for an "evolving Constitution."

Kudos should go to Indiana Representative Mark Souder for addressing the 109th Congress recently. He stated that "True faith fills one's soul. It is our core being. We should not abandon faith at the door to the House floor. We should not leave the Holy Spirit in the cloakroom." Thank you, Mark Souder, for exercising your First Amendment rights; you expressed my sentiments exactly.

Is it Illegal to Teach the Bible in Public Schools?

Ask the next person you meet what they think about the idea of teaching the Bible in public schools. Some will become indignant, and respond with statements such as "Public schools are not the place to indoctrinate students into a particular religion." Others will say it would violate the "separation of church and state" principle (not found, incidentally, in the Constitution or any other founding legal document of these United States). Some will add it's only appropriate for private schools, not public ones. Some will say it's a good idea to improve morals, but will quickly add it is illegal. Everyone knows that back in 1963 atheist Madeline Murray O'Hare won her case in the Supreme Court, which resulted in the removal of prayer and Bible teaching from public schools. A few will enthusiastically support the idea but are typically quick to say it doesn't stand a snowball's chance in a very hot place of passing legal requirements, especially with watchdog groups around like the ACLU and the People For The American Way.

The strange thing is that the above mental paradigm is patently false, and hardly anyone reports the unvarnished facts. For starters, that paradigm contradicts present reality. A public school course entitled "The Bible as History and Literature" is currently being taught during school hours for credit in over 1,100 public high schools in over 300 school districts in 35 states in our nation. That course was developed by the National Council on Bible Curriculum in Public Schools (NCBCPS). Those states include California, Alaska, Pennsylvania, Florida, and others far outside the perceived "Bible Belt" of the United States.

That paradigm is false according to attorney's opinions. The American Family Association's attorney Steve Crampton asserted in the Sept. 12, 2005 issue of *Citizenlink* that the Supreme Court did not ban the Bible from public schools totally, only the teaching of particular church doctrine. The First Amendment Center's Charles Haynes stated (*AGAPE Press*, 2005) that the Supreme Court decision bans using the Bible for indoctrination or devotional purposes, but allows the teaching of the Bible for literary value. The Alliance Defense Fund's Mike Johnson noted (*WorldNetDaily*, 2005) that the ACLU frequently challenges NCBCPS curriculum, but have been successful in only one instance in 1998 when certain elements of fundamentalist Christian belief were added to the literature. The ACLU hasn't won a case since those were removed.

That paradigm is false according to good educational standards, endorsed by the very ones we have ignored in the debate – high school teachers. A survey of combined public and private high school teachers by the Bible Literacy Project found that "Nine our of ten teachers who participated argued that knowledge of the Bible is crucial for a good education; 40 out of 41 teachers said Biblical literacy is an educational advantage."[1] Those results are not tainted, because they are corroborated by a recent Gallup poll of high school English teachers, which found that an astounding 98% of them agreed with the "distinct educational advantage" aspect of the question. English teachers point out that there are so many metaphors and phrases that stump students who have no knowledge of Biblical literature, such as "walk on water," "the golden rule," "the widow's mite," "30 pieces of silver," "washing your hands" of a situation, etc. English teachers are now being supported in their view by an unlikely ally – traditionally liberal major newspaper editorial writers. David Galernter wrote in the *Los Angeles Times* (reported in *Breakpoint*, Sept. 28, 2005) "Can you understand American culture without knowing the biblical context of 'covenant,' 'promised land,' 'shining city on a hill'?" That same *Breakpoint* issue entitled "Attacking Cultural Illiteracy: The Bible and Its Influence" also quoted an editorial writer for the *Chicago Tribune* who stated "Trying to understand American literature and history without some knowledge of the Bible is like trying to make sense of the ocean despite a complete ignorance of fish."

That paradigm is also wrong by historical example. Our nation's first public school textbooks, such as Webster's Blue-Backed Speller, were rife with scriptural quotations and stories. Nary was a question raised as to "Constitutionality." That concern only came into play through liberal political correctness dogma of "not wanting to offend anyone." It's a shame that liberal groups have put the scare into some school administrators about including "The Bible as Literature" courses in their curriculum. Apparently it's OK to teach our children about every world religion and culture except our own. I smell an educational revolt as the public becomes aware of that incongruity.

Neither Theocracy nor Democracy

The Democratic Party used to be the party that loudly and staunchly defended the strict "separation of church and state." They had a definite "secularist" predisposition in philosophy that lodged in the public's perception, and that perception worked against them in the last Presidential election – the so called "God Gap." They still believe in the separation of church and state, but are working overtime to close that "God Gap." In listening to the top Democratic contenders one might get the impression an old fashioned revival is going on.

Senator Hillary Clinton references her faith frequently, and has testified to the same on CNN. Barack Obama holds his "faith forums" and makes statements that sound as though they came straight out of a conservative think tank's policy playbook: "Secularists are wrong when they ask believers to leave their religion at the door before entering the public square."[2] Again he stole a line from religious conservatives by proclaiming "To say that men and women should not inject their 'personal morality' into public policy debates is a practical absurdity; our law is by definition a codification of morality, much of it grounded in the Judeo-Christian tradition."

That change has not gone unnoticed in the legal profession; constitutional law professor Bruce Ledewitz at Duquesne University has written a book (American Religious Democracy) that proclaims the separation of church and state model is basically outdated.[3] His definition of "religious democracy" is simply that increasing numbers of voters go to the polls and vote the way they do for religious reasons. He notes the "God talk" that is so prevalent in both Republican and Democratic campaigns, and also points to President Bush's faith-based initiatives and the appointment of Supreme Court justices who do not cater to the strict separation of church and state model (not found in the U.S. Constitution). Court sessions will still be opened with "God save this Court" and legislatures will still open proceedings with legislative prayers. He also chides secularists who attempt to stymie the democratic process by resorting to the courts when the public and majority of legislators favor traditional marriage definitions.

Secularists object that we are headed straight into a theocracy. I don't think so. In a theocratic model, public policy is determined not by the will of the constituency but rather by religious dictators who hold ultimate power. An example would be Iran, where mullahs veto any public policy they don't like. Radical Islamists really favor the "theocracy" idea. There is no religious litmus test for candidates in our system of government, and we have the Constitution and Bill of Rights as a safeguard to prevent such abuses of power. The distrust of any one individual (or council of supreme clerics) having ultimate power actually stems directly out of Christian theology – that all of humanity is flawed with a selfish nature inclined to aggrandizing power for personal ends – basically called "sin." The distrust of kings (as in King George) and the experience of religious persecution were powerful motivators for the founding fathers of our country to establish a system of checks and balances so beautifully elucidated in our Constitution.

Neither do I think we are a true "democracy." Democracy in the old Greek conception of the term meant that everyone voted on everything. In a true democracy there are no legislators elected to represent their constituents; no Constitution; no Bill of Rights; only "mob rule" by voting. Forget about "minority rights" because they are consistently outvoted. Individual freedoms and liberty take a severe blow because whatever the majority says goes into law with no recourse to a "Bill of Rights." The concern for protecting the personal rights of individuals who may happen to disagree with us, and the desire to prevent persecution on ideological or religious grounds (or racial, gender, etc) also has precursors in Christian theology. Remembering the "stranger among you" and treating them fairly was an Old Testament directive. Loving even your enemies was Jesus' teaching in the New Testament.

Neither democracy nor theocracy is truly congruent with Christian theology (unless you consider a future theocracy headed by none other than Jesus Christ). Our Constitutional Republic is probably the closest approximation to the ideal model – allowing citizens to vote in legislators according to the dictates of their conscience (and religious beliefs) while protecting the rights of minorities. The "faith talk" and "God talk" of the Democratic contenders doesn't bother me a bit. Is it really genuine or a ploy for votes?? Hmmmmm – perhaps the subject of another article.

ISLAM AND CHRISTIANITY

Busting the Myth of Poverty-Bred Terrorists

MythBusters is a popular show on cable TV where everyday commonly-held beliefs are tested scientifically to determine their validity. The same idea might be appropriate for political or social beliefs when they run absolutely contrary to established facts. A recurring social myth that is deeply ingrained here in America is the idea that poverty in other third world countries leads directly to violence and terrorism.

The Daily Herald ran an editorial article from Scripps Howard News Service entitled "Banker to the Poor" on Oct. 23, 2005 in which the author claimed "Hopeless poverty can lead directly to unrest and violence, the enemy of peace at all levels. It is the young unemployed men of Gaza, Somalia, and Afghanistan whom one finds in the back of sawed-off pick-ups with machine guns …"[4]

French President Jacques Chirac echoed that thought in his address to the World Economic Forum where, in the typical socialist ideal of "redistributing income," he urged the richest nations to give billions to the poorest nations to reduce poverty which is the "breeding ground of terrorism."[5] That thought is a truism among left-leaning governments and the political far-left here in our country. What is missing are the facts.

The Los Angeles Times, (Oct 3, 2004) reporting on the new book *Understanding Terror Networks* by sociologist Marc Sageman, came to a very different conclusion. Sageman studied 172 mujahidin (jihad fighters) and that newspaper reported "most of the accused or convicted extremists Sageman studied were middle-class or wealthy, rather than poor, married rather than single, educated rather than illiterate." That observation held true whether they were Persian Gulf Arabs, Muslim extremists studying in Germany, or second-generation Muslim extremists living in the heavily populated immigrant communities bordering French cities. One would think Jacques Chirac would be better informed.

That same startling conclusion was reached by Scott Atran published in *Discover* magazine (Oct 2003). Studying suicide bombers specifically, Scott found them to be quite sane, of higher education than average, and of middle to higher-level class status. He stated "A surprising number have graduate degrees. They give up well-paying jobs, they give up their families, whom they really adore, to sacrifice themselves because they really believe it's the only way they're going to change the world."

Alan Krueger and Jitka Maleckova studied 129 members of Hezbollah who had died in terrorist activities against Israel from 1982 to 1994. They obtained biographical information from *al-Ahd* (a Hezbollah newspaper) and found the 129 were better educated and better-off economically on average than the general Lebanese population of comparable age.[6]

That same observation has been verified by other sources in the Middle East. Three Arab columnists (Muhammad Mah-fouz of the *Saudi Gazette;* Abdallah Rashid of *Al-Ittihad;* and Abdallah Nasser al-Faw-zan of *Al-Watan)* were surveyed by The Middle East Media and Research Institute. All three were emphatic in stating poverty was not a factor in motivating terrorists, but rather political and religious reasons.[7] Their observation is validated by looking at the terrorists' backgrounds.

That fateful day of September 11 involved nineteen hijackers, of whom fifteen were from the middle class or wealthy Saudi Arabian families. The most famous terrorist of all, Osama Bin Laden, was a billionaire. The British Muslim extremist Hassan Butt noted that Muhammad Atta, who is recognized by name among most Americans, was an architect, while "Even Osama himself, Sheikh Osama, came from wealth that I could never dream of, and he gave it all up because it had no value to him. Who can say he came from an economically deprived condition? It's rubbish." Hassan also stated that most of the university students he sits with come from wealthy families.

It's also a fact that most of the London bombers were from, at the very least, the middle class, and were also university-educated. The twenty-two year old Shehzad Tanweer, who murdered eight London residents in a suicide bombing, left behind a 121,000 British pound-estate, and that was after the funeral costs, loans and debts had been paid.

It's time for the political left to give up their cherished mantra of "poverty breeds terrorism" — it doesn't match the facts. Eliminating poverty doesn't even make the list of al-Qaida's stated objectives. Osama isn't turning green with envy at the West's prosperity; he left his billions behind and disdains Western materialism. Poverty is a virtue in Osama's book. He wants us to be more like him — back to the 8th century. Look to the religious and political realms to find out what genuinely and completely motivates terrorists.

Flushing the Quran

Imagine, if you will, that you have awakened one morning to find your home country, the good ole' USA, to be a very different place than when your head hit that pillow the night before. America has just been declared a Christian nation. All U.S. citizens are expected to be fine, upstanding, self-professing Christians, or there will be trouble ahead. All public service jobs, whether federal, state, or local, are now to be staffed by Christians only. Any U.S. citizen that admits to preferring another religion, or no religion at all, will only be allowed to apply for such jobs as street-sweeper or garbage collector. Their taxes will also be much higher than for Christian citizens. It is the same for public Universities; professors will only be hired if they profess Christianity, and the same is expected of high school teachers. The major part of grade-school curriculum will be the memorization of large sections of the Bible.

A few mosques, temples, and synagogues will still be allowed to function, but only under strict government regulation. It is now strictly forbidden to build any new ones. More importantly, it is illegal to talk to a Christian about your non-Christian religion. The penalties are severe, from long prison sentences to public floggings. The worst punishments are reserved for those unfortunate former Christians who have actually changed their religion. Interrogations, beatings, and even torture are common practice at local police stations in an effort to change the misguided person's mind. If they remain resolute, then social ostracism is the next tactic. The person's family is instructed to ban them from their household, and to tell them that they are now "dead" for all practical purposes. They even hold a mock funeral service for the unrepentant family member. No one is in the coffin, of course, but it is symbolic of the fact that no one in the family will ever speak to or acknowledge the presence of the offender again - unless, of course, they change their mind and come back to Christianity. Sometimes a relative simply murders the offender when no one is looking, knowing the local police will not investigate it.

A rather severe penalty is prescribed for those citizens who publicly insult a revered Christian leader, especially one in the Bible. Once convicted in a court of law, they are taken to the nearest hospital and their tongue is surgically removed. If the insult was directed at Jesus, then they are hanged or beheaded.

What a disgusting scenario, you say? How can anyone even imagine such a horrible state of affairs in a nation dedicated to protecting personal and religious freedoms? The sad fact is that all of the preceding discriminatory and barbaric practices are commonly found in Islamic countries, especially where Sharia Islamic Law has been established as reported in various issues of *The Voice of the Martyrs*. Horrifying stories such as these regularly come my way from Christian news services and missionary agencies that are located near Islamic countries.

That cultural difference should be kept in mind when discussing Newsweek magazine's public apology for publishing a suspect story of the supposed "desecration of the Quran" in Guantanamo Bay. Allegedly a copy of the Quran was flushed down a toilet to induce cooperation among inmates. Apparently the story was false, which makes sense to me. "Flushing" the Quran, if you've ever held that tome in your hands, is akin to flushing Webster's Unabridged Dictionary - there's just something a little fishy about that scenario. This "tempest in a toilet" has sparked bloody riots in Afghanistan, along with fiery speeches from Muslim clerics in which they call the incident "brutal torture," and demand an apology from Washington. I guess the Islamic world has forgotten that Muslim prisoners in Guantanamo Bay are given prayer rugs, prayer beads, a special diet acceptable to Muslims, and their own personal copy of the Quran.

Pardon me if I see a little hypocrisy in all that posturing in the Islamic world. I really can't imagine such a thing as a "Christian terrorist," but if I was foolish enough to start a trend by being one, and was captured in an Islamic country, I can't begin to imagine how I would be treated. If the worst that happened to me was that my personal copy of the New Testament was "flushed," I would probably fall on my knees and thank God. More than likely torture would precede the separation of my head from my shoulders.

While Muslim clerics use our free press to flog us for perceived improprieties, it should be remembered there is no such thing as a truly free press in Islamic countries ruled by Ayatollahs. *Al-Jazeera* will not be ripping the lid off the discrimination and abuse of Christian converts in Muslim society. No apologies will be forthcoming from Grand Ayatollahs. Neither should any apologies be forthcoming from Washington. In a line that sounds as though it came directly out of an old Western Cowboy movie, Muslim leaders gave Washington three days to make things right. How should we properly respond? - Take that communiqué and "flush it"!

The Crusades – Whose Fault?

Ridley Scott's newly released film "Kingdom of Heaven" promises to be a blockbuster. The Crusades have been on the public's mind ever since 9-11 when President Bush inserted his foot into his mouth by using the word "crusade" in describing our "war on terror." Former President Bill Clinton pointed towards the Crusades as a root cause of West versus East conflict. Osama Bin Laden regularly calls us "Crusaders against Islam" and recruits Muslims to fight the Christians.

The Crusades were far from being purely religious wars, but you wouldn't know it by following discussions in the major media outlets. Neither would you know that this film is a politically-correct work of fiction judging by the glowing accolades showered on it by major newspaper film critics. Kenneth Turan of *The Los Angeles Times* stated "Scott and company have gotten so accomplished at re-creating history that the results have a welcome off-handed quality, making them spectacular." *New York Times* writer Manhohla Dargis called Scott's film a "fair-minded, even-handed account on one of the least fair-minded, even-handed chapters in human history." Kirk Honeycutt of *The Hollywood Reporter* lauded the movie "as good a movie as anyone could make" and stated that Western civilization was "whipped-up by religious fervor and bitter poverty, confronted the Muslim world with both the sword and cultural arrogance." He exhorts his readers to remember that "in the conflict between Christianity and Islam, it was the Christians who picked the first fight."

The problem with such profuse accolades is that these writers did not consult the opinions of the people who know the Crusades the best - the medieval historians. Professor Jonathan Riley-Smith is a world-renown historian of the Crusades, and he has called Scott's film "rubbish" for portraying the Crusaders as bloodthirsty barbarians and the Muslims as civilized and sophisticated. Professor Jonathan Philips authored a book called *The Fourth Crusade and the Sack of Constantinople*, in which he emphatically states that the film is not historically accurate, and intentionally presents a distorted perspective. Thomas F. Madden is a Crusade historian, and he is quick to point out the common misperception of most Crusaders being religious fanatics sent by power-hungry popes to slaughter peace-loving Muslims. Contrary to the film, most Crusaders historically were wealthy landowners in Europe who gave-up everything to go on these missions; there were a select few who got rich but the overwhelming majority returned home with nothing (if they returned).

The Muslim warrior/leader Saladin is portrayed as being tolerant and magnanimous in his treatment of captured Christians. What the movie omits is Saladin's ordering of the mass execution of Christian prisoners when he defeated the Crusaders in the year 1187 at Hattin. Saladin's secretary Imad ed-Din recorded their beheadings, along with Saladin's reaction - "Saladin, his face joyful, was sitting on his dais; the unbelievers showed black despair."

The historical fact is that Islam conquered by the sword Palestine, Egypt, and Syria rather quickly since its founding. Next in line (8th century) were North Africa and Spain. By the 11th century, they had conquered Turkey (Asia Minor) and most of the old Roman Empire. Four hundred years of military expansion in which two-thirds of the Christian world at that time was subjugated is what prompted Constantinople's desperate emperor to plead with Europe's popes for help. The Crusades were a defensive war against rapidly conquering Muslim warriors. Scott's film is the latest in the PC culture wars to portray Western civilization as arrogantly and aggressively offending Muslim sensibilities. By this tactic they hope to draw unflattering parallels between those unjust Crusades and our nation's present war on terror. The events of 9-11 say otherwise, no matter how Hollywood "spins it."

A Christian Fundamentalist Jihad

Traditional Christians are being bashed again — this time by ABC's Rosie O'Donnell as she hosted *The View*. She claimed that "Radical Christianity is just as threatening as radical Islam in a country like America where we have separation of church and state."

Her claim reminded me of Sen. John Kerry's statement back during the presidential election about Christian fundamentalists being really no different than Muslim fundamentalists. There is a very real antipathy towards traditional Christians that occasionally spews from the mouths of left-leaning celebrities and politicians, and they make no effort to hide it. If comments that inflammatory were made about another segment of our population such as a minority group or gays, there would have been an immediate public outcry with calls for resignation or firing. Traditional Christians apparently remain the one legitimate minority target for inflammatory public remarks with no social consequences. Neither Rosie O'Donnell nor ABC have offered an apology, nor do they intend to.

Are fundamentalist Christians really as dangerous as radical Muslims? I suppose they could be, and here is what they would have to do to achieve such infamous equality: they could start by strapping on bombs under their suits and blowing-up innocent men, women, and children anywhere in a Christian-dominated country. They could graduate from those efforts to chopping heads off Al-Jazeera reporters who stray into Westernized nations following their profession. Hijacking airliners and crashing them into major Islamic cities or mosques is always an option, as is planting bombs on airliners from Muslim countries. The coup de maitre, of course, would be bombing fellow Christians at prayer in their churches of other denominations who are not deemed fundamental enough — the counterpart to what happens frequently in Iraq. Those rival Christians must be made to tow the fundamental line, so not only their churches but their weddings and nursing homes are worthy targets for bombing. Their stated intent would be to take over the world for Christ at the end of an AK-47 barrel along with wiping Mecca off the face of the map.

At some point or another we have to, as Ann Landers would say, "wake up and smell the coffee." What do the following historical events all have in common: The massacre of Olympic athletes at Munich in 1972; the take-over of our U.S. embassy in Iran in 1979; Americans kidnapped in Lebanon in the 1980s; our Marine barracks blown-up at Beirut in 1983; TWA flight 847 hijacked in 1985; Pan Am flight 103 bombed in 1988; the World Trade Center bombed in 1993; our embassies in Kenya and Tanzania bombed in 1998; the horrific events of 9/11/01; reporter Daniel Pearl murdered in 2002; Spanish railways bombed in 2004; London railway bombings in 2005; and last but not least the discovered plan to bomb American airliners from London in 2006.

All of these horrific acts were perpetrated by male Muslim fundamentalists between the ages of 17 and 40. Why is it our airport security screeners must randomly search eighty-year-old grandmothers and women with kids in tow — but not male passengers with obvious Arabic features and names? That common-sense method would draw gasps of horror from the left — that awful sin of racial profiling. Israel uses it and has the best security system in the world, but we can't because of political correctness.

Jesus taught his followers to be peace-loving even to the extent of loving their enemies, while the Prophet Muhammad taught subjugating or slaying the uncooperative unbelievers.[8] The political left in our country just doesn't seem to understand the difference. It's almost comical to see them progress from the "all religions are equally valid and all roads lead to heaven" philosophy of prior decades to the "Christian fundamentalists are as dangerous as Muslim fundamentalists" mantra of today.

When the pendulum swings, it swings hard. It's revealing to know that Christians who really believe the Bible and let scriptures inform them on social issues of the day are the real terrorists while jets crash and buildings blow-up. It's almost enough to make me think there is a grain of truth in that inflammatory saying "Liberalism is a form of mental illness." No, I shouldn't go there — it would be awfully impolite coming from this dangerous Christian traditionalist.

Tolerance Doesn't Require Submission

Respecting other's beliefs, customs, ethnic traditions, and religion is just about universally recognized as a trait of modern civilized behavior here in the United States. Christian church denominations who disagree on some doctrinal issues coexist peacefully in this country with freedom of religious affiliation based on individual autonomy without coercion considered to be a guaranteed right. Previous decades have witnessed growing minorities of Hindu and Muslim houses of worship here in the United States. Being tolerant of peoples whose beliefs differ from your own is absolutely necessary in a multicultural society; the absence of such tolerance always results in a fragmentation of a society into increasingly hostile factions that sets the stage for violence – such as the torching of the Islamic center here in Columbia, Tennessee not long ago.

Tolerance is a word that seems to be morphing – changing its meaning so gradually as to be almost imperceptible. In past years it simply meant to respect the freedom of others to have differing customs and beliefs from your own without necessarily agreeing with them. I do not agree whatsoever with the prophet Mohammad's claims to have been inspired by God in his pronouncements recorded in the Koran; likewise for Brigham Young's claims concerning the book of Mormon. I do think

Mormons and Muslims have the right to association and worship in this country as long as they respect the surrounding culture in which they are imbedded.

The problem is that some groups view tolerance in its old-fashioned sense as almost a dirty word. Fundamentalist or radical Muslims have no interest in tolerance — everyone should submit to Allah's prophet and Sharia law. Those who resist (as in other religions) should be heavily taxed, coerced if at all possible, or actually beheaded depending on the situation, the strength of "unbelievers" opposition, and which particular verses in the Koran the radicals wish to emphasize. One of their strategies (as in Europe) is to increase their minority population by immigration and having large families (no contraception) to the point of electing fundamentalist Muslim legislators in a Democratic society – a gradual power grab using the democratic process against itself.

In contrast to radical groups who have no tolerance for the concept of tolerance itself stands modern liberal groups who have assigned a new meaning to the traditional definition. Tolerance to them means not just respecting differing beliefs, but declaring them all to be equally valid, or at the very least we are supposedly incapable of (we dare not be judgmental) ascertaining which are more valid than others. "If it works for you individually then it's OK" is their motto. No one has the right to tell you it's wrong, for that would be imposing your belief system on someone else. It's the old "We're all climbing up the mountain to heaven on different roads" concept. Truth is relative to individual perception and thus impervious to value judgment. That's the mindset of much of secular academia and Hollywood.

The cardinal sin in such a modernized definition of tolerance is being intolerant – of saying that someone is wrong, misguided, or sinful. The horribleness of being intolerant then becomes the missile fired at fundamentalist or conservative Christian groups, such as in asserting that homosexuality, cohabiting without marriage, and pornography is sin, etc. Liberals equate fundamentalist Christians with fundamentalist Muslims under the "intolerant" label without realizing that there is a world of difference.

Fundamentalist Christians go by the old definition of tolerance because it stems directly from the Bible. The Gospel was to be preached everywhere but without coercion – those who rejected Jesus' claims were still to be treated in love. Doing sacrificial acts of loving service to those who do not agree with us is considered part of our Christian witness. Fundamentalist Muslims discard tolerance altogether. Coercion is clearly stated in several Koranic verses, and "loving your enemies" is nowhere to be found in the Koran. The "God of love" is the Christian conception; Allah is the God who requires complete submission – Allah is not portrayed as a "God of love."[9]

Such a startling difference is routinely ignored by most of the media, and the liberals' disdain for the very word "fundamentalist" reveals a deep-rooted intolerance for devout Christians who attempt to live out the original meaning of the word tolerance. It's time for some tolerance.

Peace-Loving versus Abrogation and Taqiyya

With all the media coverage of the proposed mosques in Murfreesboro, Tennessee locally and near "Ground Zero" in New York, and with all the surrounding controversy, it's pretty easy to get confused over whether Islam is a religion of peace hijacked by a small minority of terrorists, or whether the Quran sanctions war against the infidels. At the root of the controversy are contradictory verses in the Quran itself. There are verses which state there is no coercion in religion (2:256) on the one hand, then there are others that command Muslims to war against the infidels until they either convert or at least submit to the rule of Islam (8:39, 9:5, 9:29). The Muslims who claim to be moderate always quote the peaceful verses, while the more radical Muslims always quote the fighting verses. When people in the West point out the implications of the fighting verses they are usually told they have misinterpreted the Quran since it was revealed piecemeal over a twenty-two year period of time - - and the interpretation depends on the context surrounding Muhammad's career. An example tossed back at the West is that Christians wouldn't want to be known for advocating the stoning of adulterous women or the "eye-for-an-eye" concept of justice stated in the Old Testament.

That comparison is quite faulty and does not prove the intended point. Christians don't follow the laws of the Old Testament because they follow "Christ" – that is Jesus, about whom the Gospels were written. If that were not the case then Christians would be known as aligning themselves with orthodox Jews and only accepting the Old Testament as inspired scripture. The word "Christian" means to be "Christ-like" – following the example of Jesus Christ. The Old Testament is considered to be very useful in showing the history of God's people, great examples of faith and courage, God's divine providence and sovereignty, prophecies about both ancient Israel and the future – but it is not the rulebook that we follow in everyday living – for that we refer to Christ's teachings (and his Apostles') in the New Testament. Jesus very specifically spared the adulterous woman's life from stoning and commanded her to "sin no more"; he also overturned the "eye-for-an-eye" system of personal retaliation to the "turn-the-other-cheek" precept for loving one's enemy. Christians believe in being merciful and forgiving, likewise.

Reconciling contradictory verses in the Quran and determining which ones should be codified into Sharia law, have resulted in the "doctrine of abrogation." The idea here is that verses written late in Muhammad's career cancel out the earlier verses whenever there is a contradiction. Many scholars point out the reason for the contradictions: Islam in its infancy was far outnumbered by the "infidels" next door to them in Mecca, so peaceful coexistence was necessary. Later on when Muslims had grown in numbers and military strength after moving to Medina in 622, verses were written about going on the offensive. The verses over time follow a trend from passivity to passive aggression, to permission to defend oneself, to commands to fight aggressors, culminating in the commands to fight all non-Muslims (from *The Middle East Quarterly* by Raymond Ibrahim, winter 2010). Please note which verses are being abrogated according to the doctrine of abrogation. The earlier peaceful verses are being cancelled in favor of the "fight the infidel" later verses – and that you won't hear on your CBS evening news.

Complicating this whole debate is the Muslim policy of "*taqiyya*" – a policy of lying to non-believers initially for self-preservation, but which has come to be used by several Muslim groups as permission to lie to Westerners in order to buy time and strengthen Muslim communities for the inevitable conflict. It is derived from Quran 3:28 and Muhammad's close companion Abu Darda who stated "Let us grin in the face of some people while our hearts curse them." Former Islamic professor at the University of Beirut, Sami Mukaram, has stated "Taqiyya is very prevalent in Islamic politics, especially in the modern era."[10] Allah himself is seen (by default since he supposedly inspired these verses) as the best "*makar*" – the best "deceiver" or "schemer" in the promotion of Islam. That is in stark contrast to the Christian God who is always "Truth" and in whom there is no deceit.

The next time you hear the Quran quoted about how Islam is a religion of peace reflect just a moment on the concepts of "*taqiyya*" and the "doctrine of abrogation." Pardon me if I'm not drinking the Kool Aid of this current administration's "Let's just realize that the huge majority of Muslims are peace loving and we all worship the same God anyways" media blitz. I'm just too politically incorrect and Biblically grounded to be good at *taqiyya*.

SCIENCE AND THE BIBLE

Science and Christian Belief — Incompatible?

Dr. Spock of *Star Trek* fame was my hero as a child. It didn't matter that he was a fictional character in the TV science fiction series, it was the idea he represented — pure logic unaffected by the vagaries of human emotions. Dr. Spock was of course the chief science officer aboard the starship Enterprise. He possessed that purely logic-driven mind that drew on extensive formal training in the sciences to offer invaluable advice for all the problems encountered in their ongoing mission (with a little occasional help from the ship's massive computer memory).

I was fascinated by the idea of exploring our vast universe, fascinated with the idea of "other species" out there in other star systems, especially fascinated with Dr. Spock. Some of my earliest memories as a child involve watching the original black and white series with my maternal grandfather — his favorite show as well. He got away with treating me to something forbidden at home — milk and sugar in a small cup with a smidgen of coffee. Sitting with pawpaw and drinking heavily disguised coffee while listening to him chuckle at the latest weird alien that popped up is still one of my favorite memories.

The topsy-turvy world of hormonally induced raging emotions of adolescence was not easy to master in my teens; the concept of being able to rely solely on pure logic and reasoning had a certain appeal. I was also going through that common teenage rebellious stage of doubting anything traditional, including my religious upbringing. Science seemed an authoritative source of knowledge, so in high school I chose all those "hard science" classes that most of the other kids avoided — physics, chemistry, biology, mathematics, etc. Pursuing the same goal in college finally resulted in a degree in science rather than the arts, but something odd happened along the way — I discovered that some of my best science professors were also traditional Christians. That fact seemed like an anachronism — an unhealthy blending of old-fashioned unreliable religious belief with modern scientific knowledge. Discovering that some of the most eminent scientists were also Christians was mildly disturbing. I had somehow been led to believe that religion and the scientific mind were incompatible; discovering brilliant scientific minds who were also religiously devout was truly exploring uncharted territory for me personally. I thought I had left Christian belief far behind with those friendly but scientifically illiterate church folks of my youth.

Fast-forward some thirty years later — I've just completed a course entitled "Science and the Bible" — still an odd couple to many today, unless the former is being used to disprove the latter. My instructor was Dr. Franklin Niles, a physicist who taught at the University of Delaware and the University of Texas. He also served as a supervisory physicist for the Department of the Army's Ballistic Research Laboratory. He was awarded the Robert H. Kent Award in 1974 for being the lab's most outstanding scientist. He also has no problem integrating his faith in Christ with scientific research.

At the same time that you are reading this article, Col. Jeffrey Williams along with fellow astronaut Pavel Vinogradov from Russia are hurtling over your head in the International Space Station orbiting Earth every 92 minutes. Col. Jeffrey is the chief science officer for this mission, and also happens to be a devout Christian. Viewing the Earth from more than 250 miles up "invokes the awe and wonder of creation, and it invokes the infinite nature of the Creator" *(World* magazine, April 15, 2006). Sometime in July he plans to host a video-conference church worship service from space with Gloria Dei Lutheran, his home church.

Let's face the facts — if you still have that misconception that it is somehow inappropriate or illogical for a brilliant scientific mind to also firmly believe in Jesus Christ and scripture, you're an anachronism — stuck in a paradigm of prior decades. Your philosophical presuppositions and perhaps your emotions are clouding your judgment. In going from a bachelor's in science to studying Biblical Literature for a master's degree, I continue to be fascinated with the relationship between the two.

Getting the mainstream media out of their old-fashioned mental paradigm of a "hostile relationship" between the two is another matter. They're still reliving the Scopes Monkey Trial — not cognizant of the reconciliation between science and scripture in that area over the last few decades.

I wish the best of luck and blessings to Col. Jeffrey Williams, and although I'm not a member of his denomination, I hope to listen in on his worship service from the International Space Station. It's a paradigm-shattering new world out there.

Scientific Measurement of Religious Experience

Scientific instrumentation and religious experience usually exist in mutually exclusive spheres, but sometimes they have a way of coming together. That happened in 1970 when a scientist by the name of Dr. N. Jerome Stowell became interested in what happens inside the human brain at the moment of death. Dr. Stowell and four of his colleagues set-up their "hospital room" in a large pathological laboratory equipped with their instrumentation. The patient was a lady who had terminal cancer, and with her permission, Dr. Stowell and four of his colleagues attached an electronic pick-up to her brain. When the moment of death drew near, this patient, who happened to be a Christian, started praying and praising God with heartfelt spontaneous outbursts. A magnetometer's needle suddenly moved to the right-end of its scale (calibrated at 500 points positive), and clicked on the hard stop, trying to go beyond it. By comparison, a fifty kilowatt radio broadcast station had only registered 9 points on that same scale. The results surprised Dr. Stowell, who was a devout atheist, and he decided to repeat the experiment on someone who wasn't so "positive."

An irascible man stricken with a terminal case of a social disease was the next patient, and the experiment was repeated in a research hospital. When the man became irritated at an attending nurse and began cursing her loudly, that same magnetometer registered a *negative* 500 points. Dr. Stowell was fascinated by those contrasting results and soon became a Christian. The account of those experiments was published in *Voice Magazine* of Los Angeles, California.[11] Ah, I can hear the voices of skeptical dissent already - the experiment is outdated, parameters of proper scientific controls were not rigidly adhered to, the study wasn't replicated, perhaps what was being measured was only emotional energy, and et cetera.

Fast-forward to the year 2005. The conclusion to a new scientific study has just been published from the Commission on Children at Risk - comprised of thirty-three professionals who were research scientists, children's doctors, and mental health and youth service professionals. Dartmouth Medical School, the YMCA, and the Institute for American Values were participants. The commission was studying troubles that often plague our youth, such as depression, attention deficit disorder, suicidal thoughts, anxiety, etc. During the course of that study, researchers reported the findings of scientists using a technique of brain imaging, and noticed a curious result. When subjects engaged in activities categorized as religious (such as praying or meditation), there was an increase in activity in specific activities of the brain not normally seen in ordinary talking or thinking. A startling conclusion of this commission is that the human brain is hardwired for religious experience!

That conclusion provokes some serious and deep thought. Just exactly how did the human species inherit a hardwired capacity for religious experience? That's one area that definitely separates humans from other animals. Some animals may use sticks or stones as primitive tools, and primates have been taught rudimentary communication skills through sign language, but name one animal species that exhibits "religious" behavior. Anthropologists have long noted the role that religion plays in even the most primitive of human societies. That's difficult to explain in purely naturalistic thinking. Lisa Miller, a psychologist at Columbia University, stated that "A search for spiritual relationship with the Creator may be an inherent developmental process in adolescence."[12]

I don't expect the results of that commission's study to be published widely in the mainstream media, as it runs contrary to the assumption that science and religion don't mix. I will, however, frequently attend a house of worship to do such things as sing, praise, worship, and pray to the One who put that capacity within me. As much as I love our pets and wildlife in general, that particular capacity makes me unique in His sight. It is a reflection of our being made "in His image."

Psychological Experimentation and Human Nature

If there's one thing common to human nature, it's that the overwhelming majority of us like to think of ourselves as being basically good. I've never met a single person who said "I'm a lousy, horrible, corrupt person and I'm OK with that." We tend to hide our character flaws in the back closet of our minds while evaluating our moral fiber more on our good qualities — sort of a balance scale idea with the good outweighing the bad. Another common defense mechanism is to point towards another person and say "Well, at least I'm not as bad as he is!" Of course the person being pointed at can simply replay this scenario by pointing at so and-so in prison. Those who are incarcerated are commonly heard to affirm "You know, I'm really not a bad person deep down inside." Isn't it strange how the evaluating standard is so moveable according to individual perspective?

As a student in psychology classes in the late 70s, I was fascinated by psychological experiments into the human psyche. Those findings were sometimes surprising —and even horrifying. In 1971 at Stanford's psychology building, Dr. Philip Zimbardo constructed a mock prison in the basement.[13] He divided twenty-four student volunteers randomly into either "guards" or "prisoners."

It only took a few days of role-playing before the "guards" became downright abusive. All on their own they forced "prisoners" to strip naked for degrading sexual pranks, or made them wear bags over their heads. Dr. Zimbardo had to terminate the experiment before the week was out due to the increasingly abusive behavior displayed. More than 30 years later, why are we so surprised by Abu Grahib? Lord Acton's famous statement a century ago is apropos — "Absolute power corrupts absolutely."

Another Stanford experiment became a textbook classic — undergraduate students volunteered to be part of a "Learning Experiment."[14] Students were put in charge of an electrical control panel, and were to administer small jolts of electricity to the subject on the other side of the partition whenever he answered a test question incorrectly. The white-smocked "research supervisor" instructed the students to keep turning-up the dial to administer ever-increasing jolts. Winces turned into grimaces, which turned into bloodcurdling screams. The whole thing was a ruse, of course, but the "subject" was a good actor. The "shocking" findings were that a full 2/3 of the participants, at the researcher's insistence, eventually moved that dial right past the clearly labeled "Warning-Lethal Dose" marker with accompanying screams in the background.

Social inhibitions against the abuse of power tend to evaporate quickly when there are no restraints, and that is a deep point to ponder. One of modern liberalism's foundational premises is that abusive behavior is learned from the environment. Resolve economic disparity, eliminate social injustice, and people automatically become "good." "Hogwash" says Steven Pinker, a Massachusetts Institute of Technology psychology professor. His book published in 2002, "The Blank Slate: The Modern Denial of Human Nature" effectively demolishes that faulty premise. Pinker's research showed that violence is statistically and causally unrelated to poverty, discrimination, ignorance or disease. He came to the conclusion that all of us are "flawed" to some degree — that we all possess innately, though it may be latent, the capacity to be abusive. That sounds a whole lot like the Biblical concept of an "original sin nature" — a concept thoroughly irritating to those of a liberal persuasion. Pinker is no right-wing religious fundamentalist — he is a staunch Darwinian evolutionist and thus has no theological ax to grind. There can be no accusations of right-wing bias here; the APA and psychology professors are notoriously liberal in their social views.

Are we innately good unless corrupted by a deleterious upbringing? Psychology experiments say otherwise. Not only do we need the restraining influence of civil society on the "outside," but we also need the restraining influence of the Holy Spirit on the "inside." A good non-moveable evaluating standard for morality is that of Jesus Christ; those innate skeletons that linger in the subconscious closets of our hearts can be overcome through faith in Christ. Old fashioned Bible-thumping? Perhaps, but it correlates perfectly with psychological research.

Did Galileo Discredit the Christian Conception of our Solar System?

"Twinkle, twinkle little star, how I wonder what you are" isn't just a childhood rhyme — it is a major driving force behind astronomy, cosmology, and much of science in general. Intellectual curiosity is a treasured commodity in American culture and rightly so — we enjoy a standard of living and technological expertise envied by most of the world. The desire to know "what's out there" has engendered very practical benefits such as your cell phone that depends on orbiting satellites, and that digital wristwatch that you look at several times a day — both by-products of space exploration.

Some of the more impractical realms of knowledge gained are also the most astounding to primitive peoples — our sun is just one of those little twinkling stars, and that star you wish upon may not even exist. They are so far away that when they burn out and die, the light still comes to Earth for million to billions of years. A good percentage of those stars in the night sky simply are not there any longer.

Children's science books routinely recount the saga of the first great debate over our own star — our sun. Prior to the 17th Century, everyone believed that our sun revolved around the Earth

— "rising" and "setting" just as we poetically speak of it today. Along came a new Copernican theory that the Earth actually orbited the sun, and the Italian astronomer Galileo argued for that hypothesis in his "Dialogue of Two Chief World Systems" in 1632. What happened next is usually cast in the "science versus religion" mold — the Pope issued an edict condemning Galileo of heresy, and Galileo lived out the rest of his life under house arrest in Arcetri (near Florence). Galileo has since been vindicated; the supposed religious view of the Earth as being the "center of the universe" was discredited; and everyone learned a valuable lesson of allowing science to progress unhindered by religious dogma. Wait just a minute — modern historians are saying that simplistic scenario "just ain't so."

Historian Martin Rudwick called Galileo's trial, as portrayed in the popular TV series *The Ascent of Man*, a travesty — a choice made to ignore the historical research available.[15] Giorgio de Santillana, author of the book *The Crime of Galileo*, states that it was not a confrontation between science and religion at all. The philosopher of science Phillip Frank came to the same conclusion — the real controversy was between science and Aristotelian philosophy, which had been accepted by the Catholic Church and interwoven into their theology. There is no statement in the Bible that the "sun orbits the Earth" — but it is indeed a foundational principle in Aristotelian philosophy. In that system the Earth was at the center, and all other celestial bodies revolved around it. The center was not a special place of privilege and honor, rather it was the lowest and worst location. Physical matter was considered ignoble and evil, while the heavenly realms or spirit were considered honorable and perfect. The very center consisting of Hell and the Earth, was a place of dishonor, and the further one progressed outward through the orbits, the more superior they became.

John Brook, professor of the history of science at Lancaster University, showed that a common objection to Copernicanism in that day was that it assigned humankind an undeserved "too lofty a position" by elevating it out of the center of the universe.[15] What must be remembered is the social milieu of Galileo's day — the Catholic Church was in a fight for survival in the bloody 30 Years War with Protestants in Europe. Being against Aristotelian philosophy was seen as being against the Catholic faith and pro-Protestant.

One of the incompetent characters in Galileo's *Dialogue*, named Simplicio, was widely thought to be a dishonoring caricature of the Pope. Also, there were quite a few proven inaccuracies in Copernicus' theory, with measurements being primitive and science in its infancy. There was no official and authoritative "Academy of Science" as we have today to investigate and verify scientific hypotheses. Aristotelian philosophy was well-regarded, and Copernicus' theory was nothing but a theory.

Before one skewers Christianity as being irrational and opposed to science on Galileo grounds, as Marxist governments traditionally do, one should take the time to thoroughly investigate the cultural underpinnings of that debate. Revisionist history written in deference to one's presuppositions is worse than no history at all. Thank God for modern historians who are "letting the sun shine in" to illuminate the secularists' distortion of history in the Galileo saga.

Does Prayer Help in Mathematics?

There was an intriguing article in the Aug. 17 edition of The Daily Herald that revealed the love/ hate relationship many people had with mathematics in their school years. It is very often the case that those who say they loved it are the ones who excelled in that subject, while those who struggled with math often report hating it.

It is a phenomenon that ranks high in interest among educators today, since our country is falling behind Europe and Asia in academic achievement in math and the sciences. If you don't "get" math, then you will never "get" science, because mathematics is the language of the sciences — it has been called "The Queen of the Sciences."

I was one of those kids who for unknown reasons had an affinity for mathematics in high school. It just seemed to come easy, and I chose the toughest math classes I could find. The simple fact that there were no gray areas, and opinions or debate were irrelevant, intrigued me. If your premises were sound and your deductions and corollaries sound in procedure, then a correct answer was guaranteed. It struck me as being the closest thing to the pursuit of "pure, unarguable truth" among all my classes. In college I continued that trend, and majored in mathematics as part of a science degree. Perhaps it's the strange symbols used for many mathematical concepts that puts people off, or maybe it's the extensive use of letters in algebra that mystifies folks. I'm really not sure. I'll never forget learning to calculate in Egyptian hieroglyphics in a history of math class - there were flowers and turtles and birds all over our pages. It was after four terms of calculus that mathematics really started getting strange. I was very proficient in algebra, but abstract algebra was really mind-bending. All those treasured geometrical theorems were thrown to the wind, and "non-Euclidean geometry" was the order of the day. I got bogged down in one chapter, and simply couldn't get what it was saying. I threw the book down on the floor in an immature act of disgust, but later asked the Lord to help me do the best I could. After re-reading that chapter the next day, I discovered a key concept I had misunderstood that opened up my understanding to the rest of the book, and I finished that course with a very good grade.

The strangest and hardest class I ever had was "Elementary Topology of the Linear Continuum." I thought it far from elementary, for there was no textbook for the class. We were expected to start with a few choice definitions and theorems, and construct a whole new system of mathematics by logical deduction. The professor told us that by the end of the class we would have constructed our own textbooks. If that wasn't daunting enough, that professor was the most aloof, emotionally cold, condescending, and arrogant professor I've ever had. He sat in one of the student's desks every class and watched us struggle up at the blackboard trying to derive this new mathematical system, offering a "that's incorrect" comment every now and then. It was so rough I thought about withdrawing from the class, but once again I got down on my knees and asked the Lord to help me with it. Once again I started "getting it," and the funny thing is that by the end of that course I had proved the professor wrong mathematically on two occasions. The stuttering, the nervous hand movements, and the slightly red face seemed sweet revenge to the rest of us "peons."

I'm not going to say that being a Christian and praying for help will automatically make you a mathematical whiz. In Christian theology all of us are given certain talents and abilities as God has predetermined, and there is some wisdom to that commonplace assertion that you either "have it" or you "don't have it" when it comes to higher mathematics. Rather than a rigid dichotomy of "haves" and "have nots," it is probably more like a broad continuum from "zero talent" to "genius talent," and we all fall at different points on that continuum. Experience had taught me, however, that praying as Christians can indeed sharpen the mind and memory that God has blessed us with, and help one to delve a little deeper into that 90% of brain capability that we supposedly never use. "When all else fails, pray" has been experientially verified in my life, but hey, why make it the last thing we do?

Einstein's Theory of Relativity and Religious Relativism

Our government spends a seemingly unimaginable sum of money on the space program in the name of furthering science through zero-gravity experiments, promoting technological spin-offs, repairing satellites and the Hubble space telescope, increasing our military capabilities in space, and furthering our national prestige. Unfortunately the shuttle program also risks catastrophic failure over the simplest of things: a rubber O-ring doomed one shuttle and crew; a chunk of falling foam damaged a wing and killed seven astronauts in 2003; and lately another chunk of foam blew-off the newly redesigned fuel tank of Discovery.

The Discovery's crew has been given caulking guns and putty knives for emergency repairs on thermal tiles. Does that strike anyone as odd? Perhaps we should launch a mini-rocket up to them carrying a roll of duct tape and a small section of baling wire to be on the safe side. Now there is a big scramble at NASA over hanging strips of ceramic fabric between tiles. Perhaps we should boost our future astronauts' morale by blasting them into space wearing T-shirts that read "Give me duct tape, scissors, and a caulking gun, and I can fix anything!"

It's also quite easy to find a little humor in poking fun at newspaper reporters covering our space exploration program. Often they have very little academic training in science, especially of the "beyond earth" variety. An AP reporter in "Drooping fabric on Discovery's belly …" (in Monday's edition of *The Daily Herald*) made the observation that "astronauts have never ventured beneath their spacecraft in orbit."

Words such as "beneath, above, up, down" have very little meaning in space; they are gravity specific. They make sense on earth because objects fall "down" while gravity tugs at our feet in the "down" direction. When free-floating in space, there is nothing to tell you "which way is down" — all orientations feel the same. If Discovery orbits with the cockpit windows facing the earth, then "beneath" the shuttle would be on top of it in reference to the Earth's position. Standing on the shuttle or robotic arm is another earth-bound concept. Magnetic boots might help outside a spacecraft, and rotating a spacecraft can simulate gravity inside of it, but walking in space is really a totally different experience than the term "walking" might imply. Another oddity in space is the absence of sound because of no atmosphere (my apologies to all of you *Star Trek* fans used to the roar of passing spacecraft engines).

It was probably Albert Einstein more than anyone else who proved how "relative" a lot of our basic concepts are in physics. An asteroid blazing past you in space might actually be at rest. How do you know if you, along with the Earth and solar system, aren't zipping past that stationary asteroid on our collective way through the universe? There is no way of telling — motion is relative between objects. There is no ether filling the space of the universe allowing one to determine what is motionless and what isn't. Einstein used the constant velocity of light along with mathematical equations to prove a lot of counter-intuitive concepts.

Time itself "slows down" aboard a spacecraft that has accelerated to a very fast speed. That same spacecraft acquires more mass (gets heavier in gravity terms) the faster it goes.

Einstein's "relativizing" of such basic concepts as motion, time, and mass have been proven in scientific experiments. High-speed particle accelerators have shown that fast-moving particles take longer to decay than their counterparts at rest — their time slowed down. At high speeds the force required to make them go even faster increases exponentially — they get more massive. The shattering of such basic concepts carried over into philosophy, in which intellectual elites started poking fun at absolute standards. Common people tended to view relativity theory as destroying the importance of absolute values and standards, even religious ones. Relativism seemed to lead to subjectivism, and liberal theologies began to reflect that philosophical shift.

Einstein viewed this extension of relativity into the philosophical and religious world as a mistake — he denied being a "philosophical relativist," and attempted to distance himself from those who promoted it. Originally he didn't even like to use the term "relativity theory" because in his words it promoted "philosophical misunderstandings" — he called it instead "invariance theory" reflecting the fact that the speed of light is constant in all frames of reference.

Actually some Christian theological concepts flow quite well with Einstein's "relativity" — God works "outside" of our human time-frame reference, for "one day is with the Lord as a thousand years, and a thousand years as one day" (2 *Peter 3:8)*. Relativity in physics does not logically engender moral relativism, and Biblical literature shows that there is a God who holds humanity accountable to absolute standards.

Improbability of Life Evolving from Green Slime

Green slime — Yuck. There are probably few two-word combinations that will elicit a more negative gut-level response from people than "green slime." It's the stuff of swamps; it's what lurks in the back of some refrigerators in that forgotten three month old covered dish. It looks and feels disgusting. A few years ago toy manufacturers cashed in on this "yucky" stuff by creating "Gakk" — a slimy type of silly putty that children can gross-out their friends and parents with. It is also the stuff from which evolutionists believe that all animal, human, and plant life originated.

Yes, they say that all life sprang from that "primeval soup" by random chance back when the earth was newly formed (also by random chance, I suppose). Certain molecules "just happened" to coalesce in the right patterns to form the amino acids that later "just happened" to coalesce in the correct patterns to form proteins — the building blocks of living matter. This model for the formation of life is taken for granted in our universities; a modern scientist that does not believe in molecular evolution is looked on with suspicion by most colleagues, or is deemed influenced by some antiquated religious superstition.

Since modern molecular biological evolutionary theory is predicated on this "green slime" scenario, have you ever wondered just how likely or probable such an event would be? Probability is a realm of mathematical science, and I had two probability and statistics classes in college in which I learned more than I ever wanted to know or remember concerning random chance and the calculating of probabilities. James F. Coppedge, Ph.D., was the Director of Probability Research in Biology at Northridge, California, and he tackled the "green slime" scenario in detail in his book *Evolution: Possible or Impossible?* I won't bore you with all his intricate explanations regarding the complexity of protein molecules, but let me share his calculations with you:

"The probability of a protein molecule resulting from a chance arrangement of amino acids is 1 in 10^{287}; and for a minimum set of the required 239 protein molecules for the smallest theoretical life, the probability is 1 in 10^{119879}. It would take 10^{119841} years on the average to get a set of such proteins. That is 10^{119831} times the assumed age of the earth and is a figure with 119, 831 zeroes, enough to fill sixty pages of a book this size."

Folks, if you are like me, numbers that large don't quite register in the cranium. I start getting numbed into incomprehension once you go past the millions. Since scientific notation for large numbers is a little confusing to many people, I'll let research analyst Dr. Coppedge give you a practical example of just how large a number that actually is: "An amoeba could transport six hundred thousand trillion trillion trillion trillion universes, an atom at a time, across the diameter of the entire universe, traveling at the rate of an inch in fifteen billion years, during the time in which chance could be expected to arrange one average protein molecule."

I really don't think a person has to have a religious bone in one's body in order to seriously doubt that scenario. It is simply too improbable; it simply does not make for good common sense.

Stephen Rowland

"Green slime" will be nothing more to me than the silly putty our son used to play with, and what you get on your clothing when walking through a swamp. I'll also try to keep it out of the fridge.

Evolution is Evolving

When conservative Bible-believing church kids go off to secular college, they are often in for a shock. Evolution is taught as a necessary precursor to understanding most of the scientific disciplines. Abundant evidence is presented for an ancient earth and universe, and Charles Darwin's theory of natural selection is presented as the best explanation for evolutionary change in living organisms throughout eons of geological time.

From simple amoebas, to sea creatures, to reptiles, to mammals, to primates, to man — this is the long evolutionary chain accepted as factual science. The results are quite predictable — either the students are convinced that their treasured Biblical beliefs are ignorant, and professors and practitioners of science become the new authority figures, or they developed a somewhat schizophrenic view of life — scientists are all deceived, science and the Bible are two separate irreconcilable systems, and you are supposed to learn everything you need to get a good job while rejecting all science that indicates an ancient earth or any evolutionary change.

This polarization is still making the news today in the form of creationists vs. evolutionists in legal battles over classroom textbooks. What gets lost in all the confusion and debate on both sides is that current evolutionary theory is not the same as

Darwin proposed. Evolution is evolving. Darwin's theory was based on the "father of modern geology" Charles Lyell's principle of uniformitarianism — the idea that all of Earth's natural features have occurred over eons of time in very small and gradual steps. Mountains eventually erode to plains; sea beds eventually get uplifted to mountains through volcanic pressure or tectonic plate friction. It's just so slow we can't see it in our lifetimes.

What Lyell did for the geological world Darwin did for the biological world — evolution occurred in very small degrees over vast eras of time. Darwin's initial hecklers were not priests or pastors; they were paleontologists and other men of science. The prevailing scientific paradigm was "catastrophism" as explained by the French scientist and "father of paleontology" Baron Georges Cuvier. His theory was that the geological record showed several cataclysmic catastrophes that led to mass extinctions which were followed by the creation of new species. Lyell's uniformitarianism and Darwin's mechanism of natural selection eventually won out, and became the standard for generations of students.

What many people do not realize today is just how far from uniformitarian principles modern evolutionary theory has strayed. Professor Richard Goldschmidt, a geneticist at the University of California, has concluded that Darwinian evolution only accounts for "variations within species boundaries."[16] Eminent paleontologist Stephen Gould concurred with Goldschmidt's assessment, and stated in Paleobiology that "Darwin's synthesis as a general proposition is effectively dead, despite it's persistence as textbook orthodoxy."[17] Gould proposed a "punctuated equilibrium" theory involving groups of species that suddenly appear in history with no long chain of evolutionary links.[18] Worldwide "catastrophes" are now standard explanations by other paleontologists for mass extinctions, such as the "Permian Extinction" 245 million years ago that killed 95 percent of all species, and the "K-T Extinction"

65 million years ago that killed the dinosaurs (probably a huge meteor impact in Central America). Evolutionists are talking about "geological stasis" (curious absence of transitional forms); the "Cambrian Explosion" (sudden appearance of almost all phyla 600 million years ago with no trace of ancestors); and the "Neutral Theory" of molecular evolution — that variations in species are independent of natural selection. Apparently Cuvier's ghost has come back to haunt modern evolutionary theory with a vengeance.

When conservative Christians start noticing that modern evolutionary theory is using such terms as "catastrophes; species boundaries; sudden appearance of phyla; and absence of transitional forms (geological stasis)" and note a similarity to Biblical theology, they are met with very hot and emotional denials from the scientific community. Why? — Because it is seen as allowing the "bad science" people, the creation scientists who say that earth is only 7,000 years old, an opportunity to gain legitimacy in the public eye. Also religious explanations are taboo in evolutionary theory. Likewise, these dramatic changes are rarely mentioned in conservative churches because the mere mention of anything about evolution is "allowing the Devil a foothold in the church." There exists a pathway between these extremes, but it is ignored by both polarized camps. How can scientifically challenged creationists find middle ground with religiously intolerant evolutionists? ... *To be continued.*

The Skeleton in the Closet of Creationism

There is a new museum of natural history, albeit a rather unusual one, nearing completion here in the United States. About every two months, I receive an unsolicited little advertisement for it from the Answers in Genesis organization. The circular describes the ongoing efforts in the construction of this museum and of course solicits contributions to expedite the long anticipated opening day. The museum will feature various dinosaurs, and in one display a couple of human children are playing near a pond while two small dinosaurs nearby watch somewhat disinterestedly! Humans and dinosaurs coexisting? That's not all. One of the major points of this exhibit is that Noah saved the dinosaurs from extinction by bringing them along on the Ark — no, I'm not kidding.

This is a very serious effort by some folks to convince us that our universe and Earth in particular are only about 6,000 to 7,000 years old. What to do about all those dinosaur fossils that speak of bygone geological eras? — Simply move them into very recent Earth history, and make Noah their savior. That, in a nutshell, is the problem with creation science. Creation science was started back in the 70s by non-scientist Henry Morris, author of *Scientific Creationism*.[19] The working assumption is that *Genesis* declared the whole universe to be created only about 7,000 years ago, and so all fossil evidence must be somehow forced into that scheme.

One would think that to make major pronouncements about Earth's history one should have a degree in geology, paleontology, archaeology, Earth science, or something remotely related to the subject of investigation. Henry was a hydraulic engineer.

Creation science grew into a movement over the years with more authors with no degrees in the appropriate areas writing books amplifying this theme. Christian professors who really are scientists tried ringing the alarm bell, knowing this popular movement in many Christian denominations would eventually bring discredit to Christianity by association. An excellent example is "Science Held Hostage" by a professor of physics and two geologists at Calvin College.[20] A major tactic of creation scientists (usually a contradiction in terms) is to attempt invalidating radiometric dating methods, since these routinely date Earth rocks into the millions and sometimes 3-billion-year-old range. Speculations such as contamination from mineral leaching to "varying radioactive decay rates" in the unobservable past are proffered as credible. Another tactic in the opposite direction is to assert that God created the Earth with the "appearance of age" — 6,000 to 7,000 years ago the Earth was created with apparently millions of year-old fossils already in the ground! Why? To fool modern scientists in their pride into believing a lie! Somehow I just can't envision God as being the ultimate "trick or treater." The "Great Deceiver" role is usually reserved for Satan in Biblical literature. I'm afraid creation scientists have a "skeleton in the closet" with that argument (sorry, couldn't resist).

What's amazing to me is all the commonplace evidence readily available that is consistently ignored in creation science literature. Whole Egyptian dynasties go back 7,000 years, and the Chinese have written records of their emperors going back 10,000 years.

Radiometric dating methods have been verified by some very obvious examples. One is a certain species of desert tree that has survived up to 2,000 years. When the "tree rings" grown annually are dated, the two correlate very nicely. Another are the ice-plugs that are drilled from the Polar Regions. These have annual layers that can be counted also, and small carbon-based bits of imbedded material date very closely with the counted yearly layers.

I took a friend of mine to the Museum of Natural History at the University of Michigan, and he stood there gazing upwards in awe at the huge jaws and teeth of a T-Rex skeleton. His astonished reaction was "No way did we exist alongside those things. We would have been lunch." Am I a Christian who believes in a Creator divinely influencing the formation of our universe and Earth? I do absolutely. Do I believe in the integrity of the scriptures? Absolutely yes. Is there a way of reconciling a very ancient Earth with the first two chapters of Genesis? Hmmmm — sounds like an idea for another article.

The Middle Ground

The created "days" of the first chapter of Genesis follow a certain sequence in the development of life — from the creation of the stars (light), to Earth with its oceans and dry land, to land vegetation before the creation of mammals, to sea creatures before birds, and finally to mankind. Many people have commented on this rough sequence being almost precisely the same as what evolutionists envisage — simple life forms in the sea, plant life on earth, advanced sea creatures, reptiles, birds and mammals, and finally man — the difference being that strict evolutionists appeal to only chance, mutations, and Darwinian natural selection to fuel the process over millennia. That led some people to question whether the "days" of *Genesis* were literal 24-hour days or indefinite periods of time.

The Hebrew word for "days" in the first chapter of the Bible is transliterated "yom," "yohm," or "yowm." Biblical Expository Dictionaries will reveal that "yom" can mean variously: the daylight period; the 24-hour period; a moment of time; an indefinite time period; an age or epoch. That is the key which opens the possibility of reconciling two very different points of view between the Biblical literalists (24-hour days) and the secular evolutionists (millions of years of unguided development). The reconciliation would look something like this: God created the Earth during the Achaean Period about 4 billion years ago; primitive marine organisms in the Proterozoic Period 600 million years ago; land vegetation during the Silurian Period 430 million years ago; and so on up through the various geological ages to the relatively recent creation of homo sapiens, measured in the 10,000-year range. This represents a "middle ground" belief known as progressive creationism, which accepts microevolution (variation within species over time), but denies macroevolution (species mutating into new species).

Progressive creationists maintain their view harmonizes quite well with Harvard paleontologist Stephen Gould's "punctuated equilibrium" model — the sudden appearance of species in the fossil record would correspond to creative acts of God. It would also harmonize with the Biblical idea of species being separate and distinct. Of course, Gould would disagree, not seeing a divine influence in anything.

Even Biblical literalists and creation scientists must give some deference to the idea of microevolution. Most people realize that as different as a Great Dane is from a Teacup Poodle, all the different dog breeds came originally from one primitive mutt. Selectively breeding for those differing traits has been a human accomplishment over the last few thousand years. What dog-breeders have done with that one original mutt is what nature tends to do through environmental pressures — the most famous example being the various human races. As different as an African pygmy or Australian aborigine is from a Chinese or Nordic blond, we all came from one original pair of human beings.

Whether it is Adam and Eve or Noah and family of Biblical literalists, or the common African mother of all women proven by the biologist R.J. Berry in blood protein hemoglobin studies (made the cover of *Time Magazine*), the implications are the same: the different races developed from one original pair.[21] What defines us all as one species (human) is our ability to interbreed, just as different dogs can interbreed. Progressive creationists see this as the very definition of "species" — the ability to propagate its kind, contrasted with the inability to breed with any other species.

Looking for the "middle ground" position doesn't make anyone happy on either side of an emotionally-charged and polarizing issue. Creation scientists, defending the 24-hour day, complain that progressive creationists are giving way to the evolutionists; evolutionists complain that Gould's "punctuated equilibrium" model of evolution has been hijacked by creationists, and that a divine creative influence isn't necessary. There have been other notable efforts at harmonizing an ancient Earth with the *Genesis* account, such as the Gap Theory. It's too complicated to explain in one article, but the point to remember is that these middle ground views are worthy of investigation, and quite a few scientists and pastors find common ground here.

Gerald Schroeder's Time Relativity Solution

Every once in a while a news story (in this case on Fox News) hits squarely on my personal interest subject – Biblical literature. A theory about the earth's origins has been proffered lately in an attempt to harmonize the Biblical record of creation with the evolutionary model favored by the vast majority of scientists. That's a daunting task considering the two systems of thought have been generally regarded as irreconcilable by most folks for generations now. It was back in my grandparent's day that the Scopes Monkey Trial set the stage for eventually teaching evolutionary theory in our schools as legitimate science thus offending legions of Bible literalists ever since. The overwhelming majority of scientists claim it took roughly 15 billion years for our known universe to form from that initial "Big Bang" event while generations of Bible believers assert that God created everything in just 6 literal days.

There have been previous attempts at reconciliation – progressive creationism, the Day/Age theory, the Gap theory, theistic evolution, etc., but in the end they fail to gather large numbers of converts from both sides because of the lack of physical evidence. Biblical fundamentalists cannot grasp a "day" being anything other than a 24 hour period while scientists cannot find undisputable evidence of a "creation." Gerald Schroeder's theory by contrast looks at the two different systems of thought through the viewpoint of a past genius – Albert Einstein. It was Einstein who mathematically proved that time itself is relative to the viewpoint of the observer, and some really strange things can happen when the "observed" is traveling at a very high rate of speed nearing the speed of light (186,000 miles per second) — time itself slows down.

The example that really stunned me in college was the "twin paradox." If there was a super-fast spaceship that could whisk away one of a pair of twins at near speed of light velocity for a week or two and then return, that twin would step of the spaceship here on earth to greet his biological twin who is now decades older than him (along with everything else being aged similarly). That nightmarish fact is possible due to the "slowing down" of time for the fast-moving twin while time seemingly "speeds up" for the unfortunate earth-bound twin.

Schroeder uses that time/relativity fact to explain how God could have created our universe in 6 literal days from His point of view (the universe expanding by near speed of light velocity from the initial "Big Bang") while it appears to have taken roughly 15 billion years of tortuously slow evolutionary development from our earth-bound point of view. That view was expressed in Schroeder's book "Genesis and the Big Bang." Bible fundamentalists don't like Schroeder's view because it introduces something foreign to them by way of science – Einstein's observations about the relativity of time along with acceptance of much of evolutionary theory. Most scientists don't like Schroeder's view because it presupposes an active creator God initiating the Big Bang and fine tuning the process along the way. Thus Schroeder gets ridicule from both sides.

One thing is for sure – Schroeder is no crackpot wannabe scientist. He is a physicist who holds two Ph.D.'s from Massachusetts

Stephen Rowland

Institute of Technology, he is also a legitimate Biblical scholar and teaches at the College of Jewish Studies in Jerusalem. His theory, it seems to me, deserves ample consideration. Because of the polarization and acrimony on both sides of the creation/evolution debate, I seriously doubt his view will get the consideration it deserves. There are Christian believers in our audience who will "write me off" just because I mentioned the word "evolution" in my article (they prefer the term "evilution") – even though I'm more of a creationist. It's a subject you just don't talk about in church. That's one reason many of our Christian young people, when they go off to college to become a geologist, physicist, biologist, paleontologist, or other hard-science related discipline, eventually lose their Christianity along the way (something else you don't talk about in church). Perhaps an open and honest attitude towards the opposing side would help decelerate that trend. Now, if I could only slow down time just a bit so I can study all the books on this controversy …

Suppressing Intelligent Design

Here's a quick word association game: With which country do you associate the following phrases – ideological suppression; stifling intellectual freedom; academic censoring; ridiculing dissent; banning books; severely repressing minority academic viewpoints? Would you answer Russia, Cuba, China, or some third world country? There's a new film currently playing at the cinemas that cogently argues for the good ole' United States being the answer to that question in an academic setting when the minority viewpoint under discussion is that of intelligent design. The highly recognizable actor Ben Stein (lawyer and speechwriter for two U.S. Presidents) narrates the film "Expelled: No Intelligence Allowed." The alleged discrimination is not theoretical; tenure has been denied and careers have been derailed.

Astrobiologist Guillermo Gonzalez is an assistant professor of astronomy and physics at Iowa State University. He did some research on intelligent design that was published in *The Privileged Planet,* which was actually funded in part by his own University under auspices of the Templeton Foundation. Gonzalez was denied the all-important tenure at Iowa State in 2006, and department head honcho Eli Rosenberg publicly stated that it had nothing to do with Gonzalez's research. A different story emerged, however, in Gonzalez's tenure dossier in which Rosenberg had written, "The problem here is that Intelligent Design is not a scientific theory. The fact that Dr. Gonzalez does not understand what constitutes both science and a scientific theory disqualifies him from serving as a science educator."

Richard Sternberg is a double PhD biologist and a research fellow with the Smithsonian Institution. Richard's troubles began when he published a research paper in the scientific journal *Proceedings* which described evidence for intelligent design in the universe. Not long after that, officials from both the Smithsonian and the National Center for Science Education began a character assassination campaign against Richard in hopes of getting him fired that was so blatant it actually prompted an investigation into the matter by Congress.

There are several others. There is Professor Caroline Crocker of George Mason University who lost her job in 2004 for showing problems with Darwinian evolution and informing students that there are some scientists who see evidence for intelligent design in nature. There is Professor Scott Minnich at the University of Idaho whose support for intelligent design resulted in president Timothy White issuing an ultimatum that nothing other than Darwinian evolution could be taught in science classes. I guess that's all he could do since Scott already had tenure and couldn't be fired. Then there is Robert Marks of Baylor University who had an online Evolutionary Informatics Lab website for that college. When he committed the ultimate act of treason by suggesting that evidence for design in science could possibly be interpreted as pointing towards a creator, his Lab website was removed by Baylor University. Apparently even committed evolutionists and their labs aren't safe.

Ben Stein's movie does an outstanding job detailing some of these abuses of academic authority, and reveals the paranoiac hypersensitivity displayed by universities at the very mention of intelligent design (which they always confuse with creationism). The movie also demonstrates a clear correlation between strict Darwinism and atheism. Scientist and evolutionist Richard Dawkins, who authored *The God Delusion*, was interviewed and he stated that it was Darwinism more than anything else that killed what little faith he had. Ben asked Dawkins what he thought of the Old Testament God Jehovah, and the vitriol that spilled out of Dawkins is hardly worth printing in a newspaper. That was a poignant moment since Ben Stein is Jewish.

Another surprising link is that between strict Darwinism and the eugenics movement of Nazi Germany. Hitler's *Mein Kampf* contained many parallel thoughts of Darwinist theory which was then applied to the human race, and Darwin's *The Descent of Man* ridiculed having asylums for the insane, taking care of the chronically sick, and even smallpox vaccinations since such compassion allowed for "weak members of civilized society" to breed.

If you're not the type of person who breaks out into hives and hyperventilates at the very mention of those two words intelligent design, then I would highly recommend taking a look at this movie. It's a real eye-opener of the "barricade mentality" that exists in evolutionary grounded science classes at the university level, and the viciousness with which anything that questions that paradigm gets squashed. I've heard that intelligent design gets a fairer hearing in Russia.

Earth — Tailor Made for Homo Sapiens

"All we are is dust in the wind…" was the lyric in the popular song "Dust in the Wind" by Kansas back in 1977. Rather than being the "center of the universe" — the object of intense divine interest of a Creator — we are located on an obscure planet on one of the spiral arms of our Milky Way galaxy out on the periphery of the universe. Our Earth is probably just one of millions of planets scattered throughout the universe, with nothing particularly special or unique about it.

The view of our Earth and its inhabitants as being quite insignificant in the total universe context of things was actually a mainstream idea of science. I used the verb "was" because that idea has changed radically since the '60s, with new astronomical evidence and cosmological deductions. It was back in 1966 that Carl Sagan, Losef Shklovskii, and Frank Drake attempted to calculate just how probable life was elsewhere in the universe by taking into consideration two very critical factors: the-type of star that we have in our sun, and the precise distance that Earth is from our sun.

We are very fortunate to have our yellow sun — if it were any redder or bluer in the other spectral direction, then photosynthesis in plants would grind to a halt. No photosynthesis means no plants which means no humans. If our Earth were slightly closer to our sun it would be too hot for our water cycle (boiling off into the atmosphere); if slightly farther away, it would be too cold (water frozen). It would only take a 2 percent variation to extinguish life on earth.

Carl Sagan and company calculated that only 0.001 percent of all stars in the universe would meet these two requirements. Since that time many other critically limiting factors have been found. In 1993 George Wetherel of the Carnegie Institute discovered that we humans wouldn't be here if Jupiter didn't exist. A large planet with massive gravity is critically necessary in our solar system because it sucks in meteorites. No Jupiter would mean that earth would be bombarded a thousand times more with meteorites, such as the one that was the dinosaur killer on the Yucatan Peninsula of Mexico (Chicxulub Crater).

Another discovery —- if our sun were any larger, its burning rate would be erratic and much too fast to permit life on Earth. A sun any smaller would necessitate an Earth orbit closer to the sun to maintain proper temperature. The problem with that is an increased tidal interaction between the two would lengthen earth's rotation period from 24 hours to several months — as with Venus and Mercury — which brings us to the next discovery:

The 24-hour rotation period is critical also. If it were shorter, the atmospheric winds would howl at unbearable velocities. Any longer rotational period would allow for night/day temperatures to reach extremes, thus making earth unfit for life.

Neither would we be here without our perfectly-sized moon. The moon's gravitational pull plays a critical role in such things as cleansing coastal waters (tides), replacing sea water nutrients, and stabilizing the axial tilt of our earth (necessary to avoid extremes in climate). If the moon were any smaller (like other planets' moons), this effect would not be realized. A larger moon with more gravity would be catastrophic.

The trend of newly discovered critically-limiting factors has been on the upswing. Since the two known in 1966, there were eight factors known in 1970, 23 in 1980, 30 in 1990, to the present 40 today. The astronomer Hugh Ross, Ph.D., has proffered the latest calculation: "Much fewer than a trillionth of a trillionth of a trillionth of a trillionth of a percent of all stars could possibly possess, without divine intervention, a planet capable of sustaining advanced life."[22]

So, where does that leave us in the total scheme of things, universally speaking? Very privileged and unique — a view which is very amenable to the Judeo-Christian conceptual view of Earth being a special creation of God. "The heavens declare the glory of God; the skies proclaim the work of his hands" *(Psalms 19:1)* may be much more than simple Biblical poetry — it well may be astronomical fact. Of course, you won't hear Carl Sagan say that, but I'm a person who tends to judge by evidence — and it keeps growing decade by decade.

RACISM AND CHRISTIANITY

Racism in the Church

My wife and I decided to attend the play *Jesus Can Work It Out!* last Saturday at the Church of God on East Eighth Street, which was packed by the time the play started. We walked in and sat on the second row; there were two other Caucasian folks there plus our friends sitting with us who were Hispanic. Funny how you notice things like that when you are in the minority. The play was very humorous while touching on common social problems often seen in churches – gossipers, jealousy, factions for and against a new pastor, and the occasional (and usually rare, thank God) romantic "affair" that regrettably happens between parishioners already married. The necessity of forgiveness and showing love to those who have sinned was the basic moral portrayed – rather effectively and with a good dose of comedic shtick along the way. It had been a long time since I had been in a black church, and I must say that there are a couple of things they do better than most others – their preachers know how to speak to your emotions as well as your intellect; their worship is vibrant, expressive, emotional, and rhythmic. We were made to feel most welcome.

I think we have come a long way in race relations regarding our churches from decades past, but the vestiges remain most evident, in my opinion, in the white churches. My wife Susan had adopted a black infant just a few days old 18 years ago and raised that baby as her own. She has told me stories of how she would be looking for a new church to attend after moving to Tennessee from Indiana. They would walk into a church and sit down – and sometimes the white folks on the same pew would glance their way with a look of horror, assume that Susan had an affair with a black man, and would actually get up out of the pew and move away. She had to go through a few churches before finding one that wasn't so judgmental. We have also heard first-hand accounts of black people visiting local white churches being told after the service that their visit was appreciated but "We hope that you eventually find a home church with your own kind." I can't imagine a more prejudiced "welcome" than that.

In my church we have a young black teenager who plays the bass guitar along with about five or six other blacks who attend on a pretty regular basis; our pastor has made it clear that racial prejudice will not be tolerated in his church. There are still some white folks here in Columbia who think such "tolerant" attitudes are simply awful – that black folks should stay on their side of town and in their own churches. If these white folks had their way blacks would have to stay in their schools and stay in their restaurants also. When it comes to Hispanics, they usually are not quite as prejudiced as long as they are not illegals and speak English. The same goes for folks from India or the Orient. If they are from the northern European nations, then they are quite all right, even though they speak another language. Swedes, Norwegians, Danes – they are fine and dandy even if they don't know a word of English. See any bad logic in this? I think it's more or less the skin tone that elicits that prejudicial feeling.

I've heard several white preachers voice the hope that one day their community would be in total acceptance of a racially integrated church – even their church. I agree with the sentiment but doubt the plausibility (even though there are a few exceptions – there are a few fully integrated churches out there.) For one thing, there is a fly in the perfume that spoils even the best of attempts towards integration – the fear many people have about interracial marriages. They know that if black families start attending their church, then there is a possibility that their kids or grandkids just might have a crush on another kid of a different color – and that they simply cannot abide. Another problem is that many minorities actually enjoy fellowshipping with, and attending church with, other folks within their minority group. Immigrating Koreans tend to form Korean churches – the same with immigrating Poles, Japanese, Mexicans, etc. A third problem is that very often those minorities hope to continue their ethnic identity as a distinct culture – and prefer that their progeny marry within their ethnicity to facilitate that effort. A preference for "homogenous marriages" can be strong on both sides of the ethnic divide.

The one thing I'm dead sure about is that we should genuinely welcome anyone, regardless of race, into our church services if they desire to be there. If you don't like that, you will have to take up your argument with Jesus, who told us to love everyone – not just everyone of your same skin color. News flash – you won't win your argument. Sometimes I think that if Jesus Himself visited our churches, He often wouldn't feel very welcome – after all, He looks nothing like those white "Anglicized" paintings we often see. He was that olive-skinned Middle Eastern Arabic-looking fellow wearing a robe and sporting a beard. He would make us nervous.

Interracial Marriage

A very special speaker graced the pulpit of New Life Church last Sunday morning. The Hicks family was visiting from Japan, and Phillip Hicks was the speaker. Phillip had served in the armed forces in Japan and while there had fallen in love with a young Japanese woman. Marriage soon followed, but troubles followed also. Phillip was living a self-indulgent lifestyle and had become addicted to drugs. A personal downward spiral resulted in his new bride threatening divorce, which didn't change until a Japanese pastor from Hiroshima talked to Phillip about changing his life through faith in Jesus Christ. Phillip committed his life to Christ, broke the drug habit, and preserved his marriage. Following a call of God upon his life led to Phillip entering the ministry, and he now pastors a church in Japan. Phillip now reverently refers to that Hiroshima pastor as a "Jesus in Japanese skin." Seeing the visual images of happy Japanese faces on the video presentation lent an international flavor to the atmosphere, as did the Israeli flag mounted on the wall with the words "Pray for the peace of Jerusalem" emblazoned on it. There is racial diversity in this non-denominational church; members of African descent are in the choir, serving as ushers, and part of the seated congregation. That is an exception to the norm; most churches in the United States are segregated by race or nationality.

The "separate but equal" policy as a model for racial relations has long since been abandoned in regard to public schools, but it still pretty much holds in churches. American pastors in years past were hoping that arriving immigrants would flood into their churches, but they had a tendency to establish their own Korean-speaking churches, Vietnamese churches, etc. Churches, much like U.S. residential neighborhoods, tend to remind one of a "tossed salad" rather than a "melting pot." I'm not sure that is automatically a bad thing - people have a natural tendency to look for social and emotional support from others who seem to be more like them, and language, national customs, and race tend to accentuate that tendency. Pride in ethnicity also tends to hold people together.

A white American who marries an Oriental usually doesn't encounter much social resistance from others, and likewise if the espoused is an Italian, Spaniard, or other European nationality. There might be a little social friction if the bride is Mexican, American Indian, or Philippino, but not much. There is a range of other countries and skin colors that gradually range from "tan" to what we call "black," and the social disapproval from many people comes in strongest at the "white/black" end of that range. Interracial marriage is a touchy subject with many people in our area of the country, and I've discovered that it is often the root of the opposition to the idea of an "integrated" church. The fear is that young people of differing races might take a liking to each other as they grow up together in church. What I find interesting is that gradual shading in colors; there is no sharp black/white dichotomy - that is a figment of our imagination. One fellow held a piece of white paper next to his skin and noted that he wasn't really "white"; another looked at the heel of his dress shoe and observed he wasn't really "black"; perhaps we're closer than we think. We all bleed red, and a literal reading of Genesis reveals that all races sprang from one original family. The very same religiously devout people who view interracial marriage as wrong have trouble knowing exactly where to draw that precise boundary line amidst all the varying shades of different nationalities. I've never heard chapter and verse cited to support their view, but I have noticed a few facts in biblical literature that calls for tolerance: Timothy's devout Jewish mother was married to a Greek; Joseph married an Egyptian; Moses' second wife was a Cushite (Ethiopian or Nubian). When Moses' sister Miriam complained about the marriage, she was stricken with leprosy (Numbers 12). Those despised half-breed Samaritans were welcomed with open arms by Jesus. I really doubt that heaven's neighborhoods are segregated.

Phillip and his wife make a lovely couple, and I wish them and their church in Japan God-speed. The New Testament does have some words of advice for Christians contemplating marriage: they should "marry in-the-Lord" (1 Cor. 7:39; 2 Cor. 6:14-15). In other words believers should marry believers. That makes for good common sense, shared core values increase the probability for good marital stability. What should really raise our eyebrows is when that advice is not followed. Many has been the heartbreak of a young Christian girl marrying an unbelieving fellow, thinking she can change him - but that's a different story. Only God can change stubborn hearts, and I'm glad Phillip listened to his "Jesus in Japanese skin." Racial prejudice has no place in the Christian religion, and I really like that anti-Semite busting bumper-sticker I saw recently that stated "My boss is a Jewish carpenter."

Martin Luther King Jr. and Christian Social Action

I was a 10-year-old school crossing guard for Van Slyke Elementary school and proud of it. My responsibility was to don the bright orange safety vest immediately after school hours and stand at the end of the drive assisting my schoolmates in crossing Maple Avenue. As an older and wiser fifth-grader (sixth graders went to junior high), it felt empowering to be given that road-crossing responsibility. After the last straggler had crossed the street, I would walk about 1 1/2 miles to my home. Today we would shudder at the thought of elementary kids serving as crossing guards and would equally disapprove of their walking home down city streets all alone.

That was a different era back in 1968, but one particular day that year — April 4th — would prove to be very different. When I arrived home, my parents told me to stay off the streets. Martin Luther King, Jr., has been assassinated and there are shots being fired in black neighborhoods. I had no idea who this King fellow was, but I could sense the anxiety in my mother's voice. Years later when I learned about the admirable role Martin Luther King, Jr., played in the civil rights movement, it seemed ironic that violent riots had broken-out across the country at his assassination, though Martin Luther had so eloquently advocated and effectively modeled the principle of non-violent civil disobedience.

King's accomplishments are legendary. When Mrs. Rosa Parks refused to give up her seat and move to the back of the bus in 1955, King organized the boycott of segregated Montgomery city buses. Those buses were desegregated about a year later and King became recognized as a civil rights leader. King led the 1963 Birmingham protest march and also the March on Washington with more than 200,000 participants. It was there at the Lincoln Memorial that he delivered his famous "I have a Dream" speech and achieved worldwide fame. The following year brought two very high honors: King made the cover of TIME magazine as "Man of the Year" and also won the Nobel Peace Prize.

Sometimes overlooked is the role that King's Christian faith played in his life. King had earned a bachelor's degree in 1951 from Crozer Theological Seminary, and pastored his first church, Dexter Avenue Baptist Church of Montgomery, Alabama, in 1954. It was the local black clergy that led the Montgomery school bus boycott in 1955. King organized the Southern Christian Leadership Conference and co-pastored the Ebenezer Baptist Church of Atlanta in 1960.

It was the black churches that played the leading role of the civil rights movement, and "It was through the sermon that Dr. Martin Luther King, Jr., inspired popular support for the civil rights movement in the 1960s" Winthrop Hudson and John Corrigan wrote in their 1999 book, *Religion in America*. There were no clear lines of demarcation between the pulpit and politics; King's "theology of racial reconciliation" employed the techniques of public marches on capitals, boycotts, sit-ins, demonstrations, picket lines and voter registration drives. Evangelist Billy Graham helped in this endeavor by desegregating his crusades and hiring the first black minister on his staff. Support for desegregation came right from the Bible: "There is neither Jew nor Greek, slave nor free, male nor female, for you are all one in Christ Jesus" *(Galations* 3:28).

This acceptance of blurred lines between Christianity and public social action is deemed quite inappropriate today by many. The modern view is that religion should be a "private" affair — appropriate only in one's home or church on Sundays. This idea leads to a furrowed brow and a condescending attitude towards Christian groups holding meetings and saying prayers on Capitol steps. Conservative religious organizations that e-mail their members about proposed congressional bills and organize voter registration drives and voter-guides are criticized as "mixing church and state." We are supposed to keep our religious views to ourselves and let people decide for themselves in private what their views should be on those hot-button social issues. Being out-spoken publicly somehow equates to being possessed of an intolerant attitude.

We can't have it both ways. Using Christianity as a springboard for social action cannot be lauded in the civil rights movement when done by black churches then severely criticized when initiated by present day socially conservative church-based organizations. Either we have constitutionally protected religious speech or we don't. One cannot either legitimize or de-legitimize the method according to the whims of the perceived value of the outcome. Freedom of religious speech is foundational and constitutionally protected, whether it be from the pulpit or in public. The First Amendment was designed to protect religious groups from the intrusive arm of government, not to insulate government from religious speech. Freedom for one is freedom for all — let freedom reign.

Does the Bible Condone Slavery?

The young lady seemed very bright, articulate, and sincere. She was being interviewed by Channel 4 news and was being a spokesperson for her organization — one formed to help defeat the proposed "Marriage Amendment" that would be on the Nov. 7, 2006 ballot in Tennessee. She was giving the usual justifications one hears for that political position, but ended it with a startling statement: "After all, the Bible supported slavery at one time." I had heard that statement made once before. I guess it's quickly becoming the crowning point of reasoning on that side of the debate; the statement to end all argument; the final nail in the coffin. The obvious implication is that Christians or traditionalists cannot logically support the proposed Marriage Amendment on the basis of a Judeo-Christian heritage because the Bible once supported the institution of slavery. Everyone now agrees that human slavery was a terrible evil, so if the Bible supported such a practice, how can you trust it on any other social issue?

There is a slight flaw in the logic. The problem once again is "cultural distance" — the same problem that fools so many people with a superficial knowledge of Biblical literature. They read verses such as "Slaves, obey your earthly masters with respect and fear, and with sincerity of heart, just as you would obey

Christ" *(Ephesians 6:5)*. Their minds immediately go to black slavery as was practiced in this nation's history, but Biblical slavery is another concept altogether.

There were several ways one could become a slave in ancient Jewish society. If a person went bankrupt and was incapable of paying debts, he could become a household servant for such time necessary to pay creditors and provide for his family. It was better than imprisonment and letting his family suffer. Another way was if a person became a thief and was caught, he was required to make restitution for the stolen amount to the tune of double, or in some cases five-fold, the stolen amount. Couldn't pay? He could become a household servant for the individual from whom he stole. Other non-felony crimes sometimes required the same household servant penalty. Another way to become a slave was through war. Wars in those days were brutal, and often there was no deference given to civilians. If you were a member of that tribe that was attacking mine, you were automatically deemed a combatant. Making household servanthood an option for war captives was considered more merciful than killing them.

This type of Jewish household servanthood was strictly regulated by Old Testament law. In contrast to the brutal slavery practiced by surrounding nations, Israelite slaves were to be treated "with kindness"; treated as a "temporary worker" or "temporary resident"; and released from their servanthood on the Year of Jubilee, while foreign servants were not to be ruled over "ruthlessly" *(Lev. 25:39-43)*. Being merciful to war captives and providing a means of restitution for criminal acts is not what modern Americans usually have in mind when one mentions slavery.

Going to another nation with the purpose of kidnapping natives and making slaves out of them is strictly prohibited as a capital-punishment sin in the Old Testament *(Exodus 21:16)*, and is labeled the sin of "men-stealing" (KJV) or "slave traders"

(NIV) in the New Testament (1 *Timothy 1:10*). That's what most people think of when hearing the word "slavery." The slave-traders in our nation who selectively quoted Biblical verses in support of their trade were depending on the common people's illiteracy and ignorance of ancient Jewish culture.

    The conclusion to the whole matter is that one cannot logically impale Christians or traditionalist in the Marriage Amendment debate on the sword of "The Bible supported slavery." The modern concept of slavery and ancient Jewish household servanthood are two very different things. It's the old saying about "comparing apples to oranges." Don't expect, however, those who oppose the Marriage Amendment to listen to such a long-winded explanation. They would rather rip a verse out of its historical and cultural context and use it as a weapon. That's the politics of the Left these days — the end justifies the means.

Christians Drove Abolition

Black slavery in American history — that degrading era where ruthless treatment of blacks as mere property was practiced and relied on economically across the nation, but especially in the South where cheap labor for cotton was needed. Thank goodness early abolitionists exposed the oppressive strictures of the Bible in sanctioning black slavery, and eventually succeeded in freeing slaves from their servitude and a racist Bible. Hey, wait a minute, that's not what is recorded in our history books.

As early as 1769, Rhode Island Congregationalists were criticizing slavery, and the Quakers were doing likewise. By 1831 Theodore Weld of Lane Theological Seminary was urging the complete abolition of slavery. Wesleyan Methodists in 1843 passed a law that no one could be a church member while being a slave owner. The Methodist General Conference passed an anti-slavery rule in 1844, and the Southern Baptist Convention did the same in 1845. Revivalist preacher and Seminary President Lyman Beecher's daughter, Harriet Beecher Stowe, wrote the classic expose of slavery in "Uncle Tom's Cabin" in 1852. To ignore the fact that slavery might not have been abolished, or abolished much later in history, if it were not for the contributions of outspoken Christians is to ignore our own American history.

"The Bible supports slavery" charge by the political left here recently also ignores a very important perspective on this issue — the black community. As might be expected, black theologians have taken a special interest in this subject — so much so that a peculiar type of theology known as "black theology" resulted. "Black theology" developed mostly in the black churches in the late 1960s, then in the seminaries in the early 70s. It looks back in history to the black "freedom fighters" such as Harriet Tubman, Nat Turner, David Walker, Sojourner Truth and others who viewed the Bible as necessary in resisting slavery. The Exodus event where Jewish slaves in Egypt were led to freedom by Moses is a foundational precept, as is Jesus' identification with the poor and oppressed.

"Black theology" is a type of "liberation theology" that views God's Word through the prism of liberation from oppression. They don't fall for the "Paul is promoting slavery" charge in *Ephesians 6:5*, knowing that accusation ignores the Christian perspective. Paul was writing not to just Roman citizens in Ephesus generally, but to Christian churches in Ephesus specifically. Christians were to have very different social relations among themselves as taught by Jesus, and that impacted their perspective on slavery which predated Christianity by thousands of years.

It was that same Paul who wrote that in Christ there is "neither Jew nor Greek, slave nor free" *(Galatians 3:28)*. That same Paul told Philemon (a slave owner) to treat his runaway slave Onesimus as a "brother" and to accept him as if he were Paul himself *(Philemon 16-17)*. The institution of brutal Roman slavery would have to be changed gradually through the spread of Christ's love; an open confrontation with Imperial Rome would have brought instant catastrophe to the fledgling Christian Church.

The major point to note here is that "black theology" is defined by all modern scholars to be very liberal in orientation.

Conservative Bible scholars would take issue with many of their presuppositions and methodologies. If liberal, not conservative, black theologians see the Bible as a stepping-stone to combating slavery in the past and racism in the future, then this recent charge by the political left falls flat on its face. The very scholars who have spent their entire lives studying this very issue have been ignored by their political liberal counterparts. Ignoring the social views and religious convictions of the black community is nothing new, however. The vast majority of the black community has always been very much opposed to "gay marriage," a fact which the political left has continually hush-hushed as they need their continuing support in elections.

I really don't think slavery and the Bible is a big current issue; you don't see it being debated anywhere on a national level. It's just a fire-bomb thrown to impugn the conservative view on the real issue coming up on the Nov. 7 ballot — the Marriage Amendment. Is it true that Jesus never said anything about homosexuality, and that implies a tacit acceptance on His part? To be continued…

"Christian" Identity Movement

It was last weekend that I noticed the yellow caution tape and police vehicles just a few streets down the road from where I live. "Oh no," I thought, "another murder." Not this time. However, someone had torched the Islamic Center. Painted on the walls were swastikas and phrases such as "white power" and "we run the world." Three men were arrested; they claimed membership in the "Christian Identity" movement.

That revelation I'm sure stumped a few folks in our area – what exactly is the "Christian Identity" movement? Some of its notable adherents have made national news before although many people may not have connected the dots to their perverted theology. They hit the national scene in 1984 when "The Order" committed several murders before being arrested by the FBI. After the Ruby Ridge confrontation in 1992, it was discovered that Randy Weaver had an association with the Christian Identity movement. The Birmingham abortion clinic and Atlanta Olympics bomber Eric Rudolph was a member, as were the arsonists who burned down those three synagogues back in 1999 in Sacramento, California. The five people who were shot at the Jewish community center in Los Angeles that same year were victims of Buford O'Neal Furrow, Jr., a Christian Identity member.

There are different groups loosely affiliated within this movement that share common racist beliefs; some of those groups are the Aryan Nations, the Church of Jesus Christ Christian, Ku Klux Klan, National Association for the Advancement of White People, The Order, the American Nazi Party, and a few lesser known ones such as Folk and Faith, Kingdom Identity Ministries, Yahweh's Truth, and the Confederate Hammerskins. What is this "theology" that motivates such murderous hatred of non-white people? Hang on to your armchairs, folks. If you are unfamiliar with these outlandish morally revolting beliefs, then the following will either leave you laughing hysterically or sobbing in disgust.

The Christian Identity movement thinks that Jews are not really Jews but are rather descendants of Turks, Mongolians, or Khazars. "Single-seedline" Identity groups think the Jews originated from the Godless Esau who sold his birthright for a bowl of beans; "dual-seedline" groups preach that the Jews resulted from Satan impregnating Eve in the Garden of Eden with the resulting child Cain being cursed by God. All Identity groups have a hatred for Jews, as they think Jews are under satanic control.

The "true Jews" in Identity thinking are the white Europeans and Americans who supposedly are the descendents of the "ten lost tribes of Israel" in the Old Testament —known as "British Israelism." The ten northern tribes were carried off into captivity by the Assyrians and supposedly migrated over the Caucasus Mountains into Europe, so if you are of the white race, then you are a member of "God's chosen people" and are a true Jew.

If you are a non-white then you're in trouble. Many Identity followers preach that the colored races (or "mud races") originated from sub-human peoples on the earth preceding Adam and Eve supposedly referred to in Genesis 1:25 as the "beasts of the field." Non-whites have no spirit and are thus incapable of being saved or born-again. Supposedly Jesus' sacrificial death only paid for the sins of white people.

Their view of the future is truly frightening. Before the Second Coming of Christ, this world will witness a huge race war with the evil Jews and non-whites attempting to exterminate God's chosen people — the white race. Christian Identity groups will be at the forefront of this war, and that's why they stockpile weapons and ammunition, foodstuffs and supplies, build bunkers out in the countryside, engage in paramilitary training and survivalist tactics, etc. Is it any wonder that FBI director Louis Freeh in 1999 warned that "With the coming of the next millennium, some religious/apocalyptic groups or individuals may turn to violence as they seek to achieve dramatic effects to fulfill their prophecies"? He specifically mentioned Christian Identity beliefs in this connection and indicated that Jews and non-whites (such as Islamic adherents) would be likely targets.

It's not just a few crazy nuts acting on simple prejudice. It's "churches" preaching a distorted, disgusting "theology" that sucks in the simple minded. Scriptures can be twisted and the Bible quoted to prove just about anything if your hatred is strong enough. What ever happened to "love your enemies"? Jesus sent his disciples out to convert not just the Israelites but also the Gentiles – the non-Jews – Hmmm. They must have spirits after all. We were ALL made in God's image, and heaven will be populated with "every tribe and language and people and nation" (Revelation 5:9). It's time to get over the senseless racial hatred.

PACIFISM AND GUN RIGHTS

Was Jesus a Pacifist?

One of the favorite charges often leveled at conservative Christians is that they mix religion and politics. Those arguing from a liberal standpoint apparently view these two categories as being mutually exclusive - the twain should never meet in public policy. The supposed impropriety of mixing the two coming from the liberal viewpoint is somewhat hypocritical - at least in the Christian realm. Liberal Christians usually support decreased military spending and often support strict gun-control policies. Since these current issues are definitely political and impinge on public policy, I find it interesting that an underlying motivation for their view often boils down to a theological reason — their conception of who Jesus was and what he taught.

Their view of Jesus is that he was always kind, loving, forgiving, and accepting of social outcasts the way they were. This is the "meek and mild" Jesus who taught us to "turn the other cheek." The Sermon on the Mount epitomizes this view, and his concern for the poor and disadvantaged of society is always emphasized. This "Prince of Peace" would never say a word to offend anyone, and his character is portrayed as a model for all mankind in getting rid of anger, aggressiveness, and judgmental attitudes. Jesus is often cast into the mold of a Mahatma Gandhi - a model for nonviolence.

Logical outgrowths of this view taken to extremes are pacifism (Christians should never use force under ANY circumstances), and universalism (everyone goes to heaven).

Conservative Christians do not deny for a second those wonderful gentle qualities portrayed in the life of Jesus (while opposing pacifism and universalism). They do, however, see a different side of Jesus portrayed in scripture that liberals don't like to talk about. They see a righteously angry Jesus physically driving cheating merchants out of the Temple by force, overturning tables and chairs in the process. Jesus used illustrations in his teachings such as "an armed man keeps his house safe" (Luke 11:21) and situations calling for the death penalty (Luke 19:27) with never a hint of moral censure for either practice. They note that God is often portrayed as being very angry at sinners in the Bible with judgment ensuing, and that Jesus called hypocritical church leaders of his day "a brood of snakes," "whitewashed tombs," and charged them with making converts who were "twice as much a son of hell as you are." They noticed that Jesus pronounced terrible destruction upon whole cities, and also stated that he personally would separate believers from unbelievers at a future "Judgment Day," and would force the unbelievers into a fiery place of eternal misery and pain. Liberals make much ado about Jesus telling his disciples to put away their swords at the beginning of his ministry, but conservatives note that Jesus told his disciples to sell their coats if necessary to purchase swords at the closing of his ministry.

Well, I don't think that Jesus was schizophrenic, and neither do I believe that there were two different "Jesus'" in the New Testament. Perusing the Bible and picking out only the qualities that fit into our preconceived philosophy only lends ammunition to those skeptics who fire the charge that the Bible can be used to support anything. In our day-to-day relationships with each other we are indeed to be as loving, forgiving, and gentle as we possibly can be. That does not preclude, however, the necessity of self-defense against thugs, or the use of police and military forces in keeping the public peace.

When Jesus rebuked Peter for cutting-off Malchus' ear at Jesus' arrest, Jesus told him to put that sword back into its place on his side. It was the wrong occasion to use a sword, and Christianity should never be propagated by force. The point is, however, that the sword did have a place - on Peter's side. Jesus didn't say "Peter, what in the world are you doing with a sword? Don't you know that goes against my teachings?" The fact that it had a proper place on Peter's side stemmed from Jesus' instructions to his disciples to purchase swords just before this incident, because Jesus was leaving them and they would no longer enjoy divine protection at all times. Lonely trails through the Judean hillsides were infamous for marauding bands of murderous thugs, and protecting oneself against them was an expected civic duty in their society. They were expected to willingly die a martyr's death for the cause of Christ at the hands of governmental leaders, but also given the means to protect themselves against bloodthirsty murderers. They were to know when to "draw the sword" and when not to. The sword in their day represented the ultimate protection available in self defense - much like a sidearm in our modern society. Those with pacifistic sympathies will puzzle over the Bible's description of Cornelius, himself a Roman Centurion — a leader of soldiers — as a "devout man," and governmental authorities who "bear not the sword in vain" as being "godly ministers."

Often this issue in our society reflects geographical biases. Urban residents who are used to a daily diet of gang related violence, armed robberies, and muggings view guns as a pernicious blight in their neighborhoods. Rural residents used to hunting and defending their crops against varmints view guns as a helpful and necessary fact of their lives. We once had a new pastor in our church from rural Oklahoma, and he kept the biggest pair of chrome-plated "Cowboy" pistols I had ever seen in his home. It wasn't even thought about twice in his area of the country. He was also the most gentle and loving pastor I ever had the privilege of sitting under. Local authorities have widely differing attitudes towards gun ownership. RV owners who keep a gun in their moving homes for protection have to buy a manual listing the gun laws in all the different states because the laws change every time they cross state lines.

Liberals are welcome to bring to the public debate table all of the statistics and accompanying arguments that they wish on this issue. When they resort to the "nonviolent Jesus" model as a defense, however, they are straying into the very taboo they charge conservatives with - mixing religion and politics. They are also guilty of picking verses to their liking.

The Middle Ground Between Pacifism and Militarism

Pacifists who refuse military service for reasons of religious belief are represented in the Christian community historically by such groups as the Quakers, Amish, and Mennonites. It's my personal opinion that most individuals in these groups are sincere and genuine Christians; I may not share their particular belief of "force is never justified," but their dedication to following Christ I would not question. The editorial espousing "Christian Pacifism" in Wednesday's edition (Feb 2005) certainly is not representative of these religious groups, for they have a very high regard for the Bible's reliability and authority. They would not agree with that author's statement that the Bible is "full of inconsistencies and contradictions," a view which seems more reminiscent of the radical, rationalistic, liberal mindset that denies the miraculous and questions the Bible's integrity. I find it strange that Chris Broussard questions the validity of non-pacifist Christianity, while casting doubt on the virgin birth, Christ's sinlessness, the Resurrection, and the internal reliability of the Bible - the very foundations of the historic Christian faith.

The validity of using force to achieve justice is not contained in a few odd-ball verses subject to "interpretation" - it is a theme which runs throughout the entire Bible. God's approval of using capital punishment to deal with premeditated murderers is found in the very first book, Genesis 9:5-6. Contrary to not demanding justice in a criminal act, God instructed his chosen people to demand restitution in Numbers 5:6-7. The intent of the whole Mosaic Law which God gave to his people was to ensure that wrong-doers *were* brought to justice, along with teaching ethical behavior. On a national level, when surrounding nations attacked Israel with the intent of defeating or annihilating them, God gave instructions to "destroy them totally, and show no mercy." (Deut.7:2) Much of Old Testament history revolves around such famous Godly heroes as Joshua, Gideon, Jephthah, Samson, David, and other warring conquerors who were mighty soldiers commissioned with the blessings of God. Wisdom literature in Ecclesiastes 3:3, 8 states that there is a proper "time to kill and a time to heal... a time for war and a time for peace." Far from being a distant or disapproving Deity, the Lord said his intent was to "teach his people how to war" (Judges 3:2) and was "with his people to fight their enemies" (Deut. 20:4).

The image of the "Godly soldier" does not change when moving into the New Testament. The Godly man that Jesus singled out as having greater faith than anyone else in Israel was a Roman soldier! (Matt. 8:5-10). It was Jesus himself who gave his disciples permission to carry a sword just prior to his departure (Luke 22:35-38). Moving past the gospels into Acts, we find another example given of devout, Godly man - Cornelius, who once again is a Roman soldier! (Acts 10:1-2). In the epistles we find Paul calling governmental authorities who "bear the sword not in vain" such titles as "God's ministers" and "minister of God" (Romans 13:1-6). Even common Christian believers are described with "soldier" literary allusions as in wearing the "breastplate" of righteousness, the "helmet" of salvation, using the "shield" of faith, and bearing the "sword" of the Spirit, etc. (Ephesians 6). The last book of the Bible, Revelation, depicts Jesus as the "King of Kings and Lord of Lords" who "judges and makes war" while leading the "armies of heaven" (Rev. 19).

Assuming that Jesus was promoting pacifism by his statement "If someone strikes you on the right cheek, turn to him the other also" (Matt. 5:39) is falling for a logical error based on a misunderstanding of the Greek word for "strike" (NIV) or "smite" (KJV). There are a total of nine Greek words translated "smite," and eight of them have meanings such as "beat, strike with fist or weapon, flay, cast-down, kill, or slay." The odd-ball ninth Greek term (RHAPIZO) was the one Jesus used here, and it has a different shade of meaning: "to strike with the palm of the hand" (Strong's dictionary). This term is used only twice in all the New Testament, the other usage being in Matthew 26:67 -"others slapped him" (NIV) or "smote him with the palms of their hands" (KJV). There is a big difference between an open palm and a closed fist - the difference between a slap and a punch; an insult versus an attack with intent to injure. The former Christians are to take in humility; the latter is grounds for self-defense.

Chris' second example of "giving away your cloak" (Matt. 5:40) ignores the literary context. It's not a thief here, but rather someone who is legitimately *suing* you in a court of Law. The third example of "going the extra mile" (Matt. 5:41) ignores the historical/cultural context. It was Roman custom to require local citizens to accompany and assist official government dispatches by courier. To refuse forced service in transport by Caesar's authority was considered an offence to the King. The hated Roman conquerors were bitterly viewed as enemies by 1st century inhabitants of the Holy Land, but Rome now represented governmental authority to keep the peace, and Christians were expected to comply cheerfully.

Just about any viewpoint can be taken to extremes. Hawkish, war-loving "Christians" who enjoy subduing other nations just for the thrill of it, or who force Christianity upon others by sword or gun, as in the Crusades or Inquisition, are a shameful aberration from true Christianity. At the other extreme are radical pacifists who advocate abolishing our military and police forces, making us doormats for thugs. That is likewise a distortion of true Christian doctrine. The balanced viewpoint is in the middle, and I'm personally very proud of our nation's Christian police officers and military personnel. God bless them.

Handgun Permits – Not for Christians?

With all the talk in the news lately about publishing the names of gun-carry permit holders (or passing a bill to make carry permits illegal), I was struck by the perception that apparently many people have — that permit holders are to be viewed with suspicion. There was the editorial by *The Johnson City Press* appearing in *The Daily Herald* (March 3, 2009) that made a wild unsubstantiated assertion of permit holders being more likely to commit crime with their handgun than criminals targeting permit holder's homes for burglary. That editorial also trumpeted the dangers of felons getting carry permits.

I had the opportunity recently to hear a veteran member of the Columbia Police department speak on this topic. I'll preserve his anonymity by calling him "Bill" for reasons soon to be evident. Bill has been involved in several gunfights with thugs over the years in his career; he will be quick to tell you that over 92% of permit carrying citizens are not the ones you should be suspicious of. Yes, there have been problems with the permit process that unfortunately allowed some felons to obtain permits; that obviously should be error-proofed and stopped. It's time, however, for a little common sense here. Do you really think that a convicted felon who could care less about the law is going to refrain from carrying a handgun because he didn't get a permit? It's illegal for a convicted felon to have a handgun in the first place, but they get them any time they want on the black market. Are they going to be concerned about that piece of paper?

Officer Bill is very much in favor of citizens having the right to legally arm themselves, and lately well over 1,600 Maury County residents have done just that – and training classes are booked into the future. Robberies and shootings have been splashed across the front page of *The Daily Herald* for months now and people are getting fed-up with deranged druggies and heartless gang-bangers creating havoc in our community.

People don't feel safe anymore and they have good reason to feel that way. If a thug is waving a gun at you, calling 911 will probably get you shot. A violent confrontation is usually over by the time the police arrive. Add to that the fact that quite a few police officers are not very skilled with handgun accuracy themselves; training for accuracy has never been a high priority in the budget for officer training. Bill stated that some police officers have trouble even hitting the target at the firing range – and they are the ones we are depending on to protect us.

Those who view permit carrying citizens suspiciously and want their names listed in the newspaper just like those who have been arrested for some offense need a reality check. There are ladies with restraining orders who have carry permits and are in fear for their very lives from unstable ex's. There are elderly folks and handicapped individuals who don't have the physical strength to defend themselves. A martial arts expert would likely lose against a gun-firing criminal.

When I think of all the various pastors who have influenced me greatly in my life, there are two who really stand out as being models of love. One was a pastor from Oklahoma who had a pair of shiny nickel-plated revolvers in his "cowboy holsters." The other is a pastor of a large church in Lewisburg who routinely carries a small handgun for protection. Both these pastors bent over backwards to help people out time and time again – they really impacted my life personally with their unconditional love. Stereotypes of carry permit holders as being unstable gun-happy nuts are just that – stereotypes.

One charge leveled against Christian carry permit holders is "What's the matter? Don't you believe that God can protect and care for you?" That faulty logic is best answered with a question: Do you pay for car and home insurance? What for? Do you routinely lock your doors? Why? Don't you believe God can take care of you? Yes, we believe God can take care of us. We also believe that God gave us a brain and expects us to protect our loved ones, and ourselves, should the unthinkable happen. It's not just non-Christians who are victimized. There are quite a few Christian men who take seriously the scripture's command to love and protect their wives and children from rapists and murderers. It's time to discard the stereotypes and abide by a principle Jesus taught: don't be so quick to judge.

"Christian" Militias?

Well, there is nothing quite like a bunch of camouflaged Michigan rednecks (I was born and raised a Michigander so I can say that) running around in the woods making plans to kill local, state, and federal officers with IED's to make me think of Easter. Too far a stretch of imagination, you say? Bear with me for a few lines.

The big news lately is that an off-beat group of Michigan militiamen who call themselves the "Hutaree" were arrested Sunday on charges of using and teaching others how to use explosives, weapons of mass destruction, and seditious conspiracy (AOL news). What really galls me personally is the "Christian militia group" designation of the AP article written by Mike Householder. What is offensive to me is not the AP article but the Hutaree's self-designation as "Christian Warriors" according to their website. My first observation while browsing through their online literature were the grammatical oddities such as using "there" for "their," "givin" for "given," and phrases such as "and not on only philosophy." These folks simply didn't graduate at the heads of their classes. Over in the "Chaplain's corner" a Hutaree brother is urging his fellow militiamen to get their souls right with God before grabbing those AK-47's for war with the anti-Christ and the devil worshipping new world order, a war which I assume will happen through those law enforcement officers and the government. "Pastor" Zulif Ruektoen expresses appreciation for the "amen corner." It's just a good old-fashioned church meeting to make one feel warm and fuzzy all over.

What was really funny was their approved link to the VOM — Voice of the Martyrs – which is a very legitimate Christian organization that speeds relief to persecuted Christians in restricted countries. VOM is adamant in urging persecuted believers not to take up arms against their totalitarian governments but rather to follow in the footsteps of their Savior, Jesus Christ, who offered no resistance whatsoever to his impending execution. That's worthy of some thought. If anyone was ever unjustly framed, it was Jesus. If anyone had a right to protest surely it was Him. Pontius Pilate and the Roman government didn't want to execute a man who did nothing but good, but the Pharisees, Sadducees, and temple priests felt their place in society was threatened by this fellow claiming to be divinity – God's only Son – and so Jesus' fate was sealed. Once again religious zealots rushed to momentous horrendous judgment where ordinary mortals feared to tread.

When Jesus was being arrested, the disciple Peter drew out his sword and smacked the high priest's servant upside the head with it – to be publicly rebuked by Jesus. Having a personal sword for defense against thugs is one thing; to serve honorably in your country's military is no where condemned by Jesus; but to use arms against official representatives of the government was specifically forbidden by Christ since it is so unlike the gospel of peace and reconciliation ushered in to our sick world by the Prince of Peace. Bear in mind that the Roman government of their day was more corrupt than ours presently.

If Jesus was truly who He claimed to be, then He could have stopped the crucifixion proceedings at any time, or as Jesus himself stated, He could have called "more than twelve legions of angels" to help Him. He went to that Cross willingly to bear our sins and reconcile us to His Father, then three days later was gloriously resurrected from the tomb – a miracle which we celebrate as Easter. The Hutarees were preparing to fight their own US government as "agents of the Anti-Christ" which is a very un-Jesus like thing to do. It's also Biblically illogical, because if you believe in a future anti-Christ spoken of in Revelation chapter 13 then you know that "He was given power to make war against the saints and to conquer them" (verse 7). Why fight the inevitable? Jesus warned his disciples that martyrdom awaited them and that they were to accept that fact – why can't the Hutarees? Don't they believe in Jesus' prediction about believers being "resurrected" someday just like Him? I didn't see anything like that discussed in their literature; I guess they didn't have time between the reconnaissance practice raids and the bomb making. Happy Easter everyone and I look forward to a resurrection someday just as my Savior was resurrected.

HOMOSEXUALITY AND CHRISTIANITY

Obama's Gay Rights Theology

Barack Obama has left no doubt in the minds of voters where he stands on gay rights. In a letter sent to several gay rights organizations, Obama made it clear that he will fight for benefits concerning "domestic partners" of federal employees; similar tax rates for both married and gay couples; affording homosexual couples the same adoption access that heterosexual couples enjoy; repeal the Defense of Marriage Act (DOMA). To refresh our memories, DOMA was not signed into law by a Republican President – it was passed back in 1996 by whopping margins of 85-14 in the Senate and 342-67 in the House and signed into law by Bill Clinton. In the 27 states where marriage protection amendments have passed, the vote averaged almost 70% in favor. Obama has placed himself well to the left of most Americans on this issue.

What really struck me as interesting was Obama's brief foray into theology. Assuming the demeanor of a scholarly Biblical exegete, Obama made the following public statement: "I don't think it (same sex union) should be called marriage, but I think that it is a legal right that they should have that is recognized by the state ... If people find that controversial then I would just refer them to the Sermon on the Mount, which I think is, in my mind, for my faith, more central than an obscure passage in Romans." I had no idea Obama possessed a degree in theology!

The lack of press coverage and commentary about that statement is revealing. Imagine just for a moment, if you will, what would have happened if Mike Huckabee had stated publicly "Romans chapter one specifically condemns homosexuality in very clear language, and that informs my political views on this issue." I think the press would have been all over that statement; political commentary in newspapers such as *The New York Times* would have been bellowing out thunderous warnings about impending theocracy. Obama's statement was buried deep within the few articles that actually mentioned it; he gets a "free pass" from intense scrutiny because he is the liberal media's darling — the charismatic second coming of John F. Kennedy with minority status.

Gay rights are "central" to the Sermon on the Mount, though homosexuality is never mentioned there? The passage in Romans (1:26-27) is "obscure" wherein lesbian and homosexual behavior is described as "shameful lusts ... unnatural relations ... indecent acts ... perversion"? It must be the Obama Revised Version he was reading out of because none of my versions read that way. Biblical scholars abide by some rather common-sense rules when it comes to obscure Biblical passages. An obscure passage is one that doesn't speak clearly or definitively about the specific subject matter being considered, thus allowing a multitude of possible interpretations. The Protestant Reformers approached obscure verses with the "Scripture interprets Scripture" principle – that is, "The entire Holy Scripture is the context and guide for understanding the particular passages of Scripture." That's a pretty simple idea – if a verse seems a little unclear then you go to all the other verses in the Bible that speaks to that same subject for help in clarification. Other books of the Bible all have a uniform witness against homosexual behavior where it is described, from the Sodom and Gomorrah episode of Genesis 19, to the death penalty law of Leviticus 20:13, to the inadmissibility of homosexuals into the Kingdom of God of 1 Corinthians 6:9-10, to the "immoral and impure sinners" description of 1 Timothy 1:9. The Roman Catholic Church approaches obscure passages by declaring its teaching magisterium to have "the mind of the Spirit" which enables them to interpret obscure passages infallibly. Sorry Obama, they see the issue the same way as Protestants. Don't look to help from the Muslims, either, for the Koran is just as adamant against homosexual behavior.

I'm having a little fun poking fun at Obama. I'm sure he claims to be no Biblical scholar; he simply does what a lot of people do – color Biblical interpretation with their presuppositions or preconceptions. That is the error of eisogesis that true scholars try to avoid – importing an outside meaning into Scripture. Biblical scholarship is all about exegesis – exporting the meaning out of Scripture. It simply brought a chuckle out of me, but the real shame is that free pass given by the media. Quite revealing, don't you think?

Genetics is the Key?

The cultural debate over homosexual marriages is currently being played out in State legislatures and courts throughout our country, and President Bush has called for a constitutional amendment defining marriage in traditional terms. The debate is a fierce one, with emotions running hot on both sides, and it is one of those issues that deeply polarizes the American public. I've noticed that both sides tend to vilify and distort the other's beliefs, somewhat akin to political mudslinging in an election year.

On the conservative side I've noticed that gays are considered to have chosen their sexual orientation despite the objections of many who assert they were born that way. Gays are viewed as rabidly focused on destroying the traditional meaning of family, and are seen as being oblivious or hostile to orthodox Christian belief in the scriptures. They are viewed as loud, pushy, and politically influential far beyond the small percentage of the population they occupy. They are caricatured as publicly flaunting their lifestyles with public displays of affection; scheming to recruit more gay inductees with public school education courses designed to portray them as socially acceptable and normal; and actively plotting the downfall of conservative Christianity.

On the gay rights side, I've noticed that conservatives are often automatically labeled homophobes and are viewed as being narrow-minded intolerant bigots desperately in need of diversity training. They assume that conservatives base their position solely on a fundamentalist understanding of scripture, and are therefore religious zealots undeserving of a public forum in debate. Conservatives are caricatured as hate-filled irrational people intent on manipulating the US constitution in order to promote discrimination.

I think the truth lies somewhere between these extremes; the crux of the debate boils down to the role that genetics plays in our sexual orientation. The gay-rights movement tends to foster the illusion that all homosexuals are genetically born with their sexual orientation hard-wired into their brains and are therefore incapable of change. That view ignores the success that several national organizations have had in helping interested homosexuals change their sexual orientation. One group is Exodus International, a non-profit organization that has over 135 branches in 17 countries. Exodus representatives have been interviewed on *60 Minutes, 20/20, Good Morning America, Time, Newsweek,* and *The Washington Post*. Jane Boyer, a former lesbian, is a board member who often represents the organization and has been happily married to her husband now for over 20 years; they have two children. She has been interviewed on *Geraldo* and *Phil Donahue*. Perhaps that sexual-orientation genetic switch is not as hard-wired in all people as the gay movement would have us believe.

On the other hand, conservatives tend to paint all homosexuals as homosexuals by choice, ignoring the percentage of program drop-outs whom were completely incapable of changing their sexual orientation, notwithstanding their high level of motivation. That drop-out rate should give pause to the argument that all homosexuality is by choice. Genetics obviously plays a role in other sexual physical aspects. Some people are born with duplicate external sexual organs, while others seemingly have none. Some are born with one ovary and one testicle – I suppose they could be charged with homosexuality no matter whom they fell in love with.

Assuming that a certain percentage of homosexuals are indeed born that way does not necessarily vitiate the conservative's point-of-view. Gay supporters would say that inborn homosexuality is evidence that God made them that way, and therefore it's useless to expect them to "put a damper" on their homosexual urges. They assert that Jesus never said anything about homosexuality, and attribute the Apostle Paul's condemning statements to cultural bias. Conservatives note that Jesus neither said anything about rape or pedophilia; the people in Rome to whom Paul was writing had already accepted homosexuality in Paul's day; and all the other biblical writers who addressed the subject universally condemned homosexuality.

It's truly amazing how many genetic disorders exist that have a direct bearing on a person's behavior and personality. Medical science acknowledges that there is a genetic link present in certain individuals and particular ethnic groups that predisposes them to alcoholism. Tourette's syndrome is a genetic disorder that influences a person to grunt, swear, or bark in public places. Most people are familiar with the multiple hand-washings and other highly repetitive routines of obsessive/compulsive individuals. What isn't so well known is that the University of British Columbia's senior scientist at Vancouver's Centre for Molecular Medicine and Therapeutics has found a genetic link to extreme aggression in mice, with human implications. Two other studies have verified this genetic link to violence in humans:

1. The University Hospital in Nijmegen found that a Dutch family prone to violent behavior had a mutation in the gene encoding the enzyme Monoamine Oxidase. It was carried on the X chromosome and only affected male members of the family.

2. A study in Finland found that many men with violent tendencies had a neurotransmitter serotonin deficiency – the lack of which has been linked to aggressive behavior.

In any of these genetically related categories, do we as a society classify them as "normal" — as being the way "God intentionally made them?" Do we frown on any social or medical intervention for these individuals? Do we encourage the acceptance of alcoholism for those possessing the alcohol gene? Do we require diversity training courses to acclimate us to the normalcy of genetically-linked aggressive behavior? Do we approve of barking in public? Should employers be required to restructure their work environment to accommodate the highly-repetitive needs of compulsive/obsessives? The answer is obviously "No." Regardless of the genetic link, we expect these individuals to seek the available social and medical help available to them to assist them in curbing these inborn impulses. These intense desires or impulses are rightfully viewed as being abnormal and counterproductive to the individual's place in society. So then why do we suddenly make a dramatic exception for genetically related homosexuality? If everyone shared this "normal" genetic "gift," human civilization would be doomed to extinction in a generation. Could it be that we live in such a sex-crazed culture that the only sin is that of denying a person free expression of their sexual impulses no matter what form it takes? That type of thinking is also rampant in the heterosexual world. Living together before marriage is now considered acceptable; teenagers having sex is considered inevitable; many support the legalization of prostitution; the American Psychological Association is no longer considering incest to be abnormal behavior; pornography is mainstream; and some argue for a lowering of the legal age of consent. Sexual expression has been enthroned as the new god in American culture, so we should not be surprised that any conservative view towards controlling impulses in that area is automatically deemed intolerant.

The conservative Christian does not have to wince or take a step backwards when the topic of genetics is tossed their way. The possible genetic component of sexual orientation is viewed impartially compared with all the other known genetic disorders that directly affect human behavior – for they are just that – unfortunate genetic *defects*. Intentionally curbing abnormal impulses is considered admirable; completely giving way to them is considered just as socially unacceptable as alcoholism, violent behavior, and barking in public. God didn't create Adam and Steve, and the traditional definition of marriage should remain so unreservedly.

Jesus Never Said Anything About It ...

With the Marriage Amendment coming up on the Nov. 7 ballot, I've heard a lot of reasons given by those who do not agree with it — it's legalizing discrimination, it's depriving gays from societal benefits due to married couples, it ignores the supposed fact that homosexuality is genetic and unalterable, it caters to homophobia, or it's mean-spirited.

Any one of those assertions could be debated at length, but another reason I've heard lately intrigues me the most, because it's a purely theological one. It goes like this: "Jesus never said anything about homosexuality." The implication is that it was a non-issue with Jesus, or that he gave tacit approval of homosexuality. Of course you never hear a good response back from those folks when people say "Yes, but neither did Jesus say anything about wife-beating, child abuse, or rape."

The first question to be raised with that statement is "How do you know?" The inaccurate presupposition implicit in that statement is that everything Jesus ever said is recorded in the Bible — a rather illogical and downright funny concept if you think about it. By that assumption Jesus never uttered a word all of his childhood until the first recorded conversation with His parents at age 12.

What we actually have in the four Gospels is a very sparse record of Jesus' statements, a fact verified by the Bible itself. *John 21:25* states that if everything about Jesus was written then "even the whole world would not have room for the books that would be written." The Old Testament that Jesus and His contemporaries studied addressed homosexual behavior very directly, and it would be odd indeed for Jesus never to have uttered a word about what he studied.

The question properly phrased would be "What method did the Gospel writers use in determining which statements by Jesus would be recorded for future posterity?" The question revolves around authorial selectivity — what was selected and why? The "what was left out" part is pretty easy to figure out theologically speaking — all of the discourse about Old Testament teachings that were commonly accepted and taught in the synagogues weekly would not have been included in the New Testament because of sheer repetition.

The New Testament didn't need an imbedded Old Testament — everyone already had that. The bulk of what was recorded was what was "new" — the speeches and casual conversation with the disciples that revealed new insights, new reflections on Old Testament concepts, all the abundant miracles that were done as never before, and the particulars about Jesus Himself that were strange indeed — the virgin birth, His resurrection, and His ascension into heaven.

What the Gospel writers were very careful to record were the debates — the disagreements with the sects that demanded strict obedience to the Old Testament Law such as the Pharisees. The Pharisees were suspicious of Jesus and His claims and were constantly trying to accuse Him of ignoring or violating "The Law."

If it were suspected that Jesus had an accommodating view of homosexuality when it was called "detestable" in *Leviticus 18:22* and was categorized as a death-penalty sin by *Leviticus 20:13*, then they would have been all over that like bees on honey. It would have been hotly debated and recorded.

The absence of any statement by Jesus on the subject indicates He did not vary from the Old Testament's condemnation of homosexuality as a serious sin. Rather than questioning the authority of Old Testament scripture, Jesus affirmed it by saying "Do not think that I have come to abolish the Law or the Prophets; I have not come to abolish them but to fulfill them" *(Matthew 5:17)*. Jesus often quoted Old Testament verses in His teachings and also referred to divine judgment on Sodom and Gomorrah on more than one occasion. Those two ancient Biblical cities were practically synonymous with homosexuality in the public's mind, and would have been a very poor example to use for divine judgment if Jesus had a different opinion about it.

It's also noteworthy that Jesus charged his disciples with carrying on His teachings, and promised that the Holy Spirit would guide and remind them of everything Jesus had taught *(John 14:26)*. The Apostle Paul called homosexuality "sinful ... sexually impure ... degrading ... shameful ... and unnatural" in *Romans 1:24-27*. That same Apostle also wrote a list of lifestyle behaviors that prevent one from inheriting eternal life in *1 Corinthians 6:9-10* which includes "homosexual offenders."

I really don't think the objectors to the Marriage Amendment are all that concerned about theology. Their purpose is to throw a seed of doubt into Christians' minds about the subject in hopes of affecting the vote. Judging by all the other states that have passed this Marriage Amendment, it's not working.

Gay Agenda Chips Away at Freedom

Freedom of expression and religion are treasured Constitutional rights in this country, but for those of traditional Christian faith, those rights are increasingly being infringed upon in one specific area — that of homosexuality. A rather poignant example is that of Matt Barber, an employee of Allstate Insurance. Matt had written his opinion that homosexuality is a sin in a personal letter on his own time, but once his employer learned of Matt's personal conviction on that matter, he was summarily fired. Apparently he was in violation of his employer's diversity clause as a condition of employment. Matt has filed a lawsuit against his former employer for religious discrimination, and in the meantime Lutheran Church Charities has set up a fund to prevent Matt and his family from losing their home through foreclosure.

Matt's case is representative of a growing conflict nationwide between traditional Christians and the current politically-correct mood of normalizing homosexuality in all facets of American society. The numbers of examples are mind-boggling. Do public elementary and middle schools have the right to promote pro-homosexuality views in sex-ed classes against the wishes of parents? Can private companies fire conservative Christians for not totally agreeing with diversity statements? Do Christian clubs on college campuses have to elect leaders who espouse the pro-gay position, or who are homosexuals themselves, because of the university's non-discrimination policies? Must Christian bookstore owners hire gays against their denomination's beliefs? How about churches and secretaries, or Christian charities and their workers? When conservative congregations break-away from their denomination over the ordination of homosexual ministers, do they legally forfeit all rights to their local church property? All of these examples have resulted in court cases lately.

In an article in last Thursday's *Daily Herald,* Thomas Munro expressed his disbelief of a "homosexual agenda" as anything real or substantial in this country. That claim seems a little dubious to me — surely anyone in the news business has heard of ACT-UP, Lambda Legal Defense and Education Fund, The National Gay and Lesbian Task Force, The Human Rights Campaign, People for the American Way, Pride Festivals, PFLAG, and other highly organized political action groups dedicated to what — nothing?

Surely everyone has heard of the state-by-state efforts to legalize homosexual marriage, which have resulted in the backlash of several state efforts to define marriage as heterosexual. Appealing to "respect for world religions" in support of the gay agenda is puzzling also. Both Jewish and Christian scriptures prohibit homosexuality; Muslims deplore it and call it "abnormal human acts;" Southeast Asian Buddhists view it as "Karmic punishment" while the Dalai Lama condemns the "inappropriateness of homosexual sex;" the Sikhs call it sinful and say it is one of the "Five Thieves" or vices; Hinduism regards sex as primarily for procreation and the Vedanta discourages homosexuality as lustful and distracting; Baha'i bans the act while maintaining that those with such tendencies must remain celibate; not to mention the Mormon's and Jehovah's Witnesses' condemnation of the gay lifestyle.

One of the favorite tactics of gay activists is to link their cause with the civil rights movement. That doesn't go over very well in the black community, a fact recognized by even the most liberal of academicians. Henry Louis Gates, Jr., chairs the African American Studies program at Harvard, and in typical liberalese he has lamented, "The black community has traditionally been homophobic." The Rev. Walter Fauntroy is the 70-year-old who was coordinator for the 1963 March on Washington in which Martin Luther King gave his famous "I Have a Dream" speech, and has promoted countless civil rights initiatives in his community and the legislature. He serves as pastor of the New Bethel Baptist Church in Washington and draws the "line in the sand" at gay marriage. His comments were, "My religious tradition says it is an abomination," and "Don't come to me asking society to attribute to a same-sex union the term 'marriage' — it's a misnomer." Fauntroy supports a constitutional amendment preserving the traditional definition of marriage.

Traditional Christians are on the verge of losing substantial rights in the freedom of expression and religion department over this very issue, right down to being fired. Just ask Matt.

Should You Have a Gay Friend?

I have an unusual friend. She is extremely kind, compassionate, and thoughtful, while working in the very high-stress United States Postal Service field of employment (They don't call it "going Postal" for nothing). That in itself is commendable but not all that unusual; I'm sure there a lot of good folks who work for USPS. She also enjoys motorcycling and looks forward to participating in Christian Motorcyclist Association rides this year if her work schedule allows for it. She attends a very conservative church. Those two together might be considered a little odd to some, but nothing really startling. She also has lived in a lesbian relationship for years, and I consider her a good friend. Considering my stance on what God's word says about homosexuality and my position as a traditional social-conservative Christian, that might be considered by many to be unusual.

I first met "Angela" when she started coming to our Bible study group on Sunday nights. She had just started attending our church and was looking for a deeper relationship with Christ and some friends to study the Bible with. The friendly social setting of meeting in our group leader's home for study is conducive to opening up personally and getting to know one another a bit better, and that's when the bombshell was dropped: Angela and

"Pamela" had been living together for years. Apparently Angela had given her heart to Jesus Christ about a year previous and had been having real reservations about her sexual relationship to Pamela based on what the scriptures say about that subject. She expressed her concern to her partner and they both agreed to simply be good friends until this question was resolved – their relationship had been platonic for several months.

That revelation left many of us in the Bible study group with that stunned "Ughhh, what do we do now?" question lingering in the back of our minds. We ended up doing what we usually do – show compassion, listen empathetically, share our fears, worries, heart's desires, (and a lot of good home cooked meals) and prayed for one another while being faithful to the truth of scripture. Overcoming that initial "yuck factor" as some people call it came home to me in a personal way.

"Hey, want to go on a motorcycle ride with me and a couple of friends to Lynchburg?" she asked me. "Sure, I'm always ready for a bike ride," so off I went with Angela and her friends. Coming back into town it was "Hey, would you like to stop by the apartment for a few minutes and meet Pamela?" Ughhh, OK. Actually it was a very pleasant visit. Pamela was a great host and I was made to feel very welcome there. Not long after that Angela and Pamela invited our Bible study group over for an outdoors barbecue cook-out at their place and the hospitality was outstanding.

Since that time Pamela decided it was best to gather her possessions and move back in with her mother (her parents were ecstatic); Angela has not missed a church service and is growing by leaps and bounds in the Christian faith; both ladies remain good friends with each other but nothing more. More surprisingly Angela is now experiencing a real desire to start dating Christian fellows. Prayer works.

Things could have been so different. What if we had turned that initial "yuck factor" into overtly expressed social distancing if not subtle hostility? What if we had given off that distinct malodorous attitude of "You're not really welcome here" which is oh-so-easy to do without ever even saying a word? We could have turned someone away from Christ and would have to answer for it on Judgment Day. That's a heavy thought.

Often it's not so much what you say but rather how you say it. People will tend to listen seriously to corrective advice from a trusted friend but rarely from a stranger. Be a friend first; Jesus was.

Angela's dad passed away a few days ago. I went to the funeral and got a big hug from Angela at church the following Sunday along with a "Thanks for being there." Her dad was a strong Christian believer, and in one of his few lucid moments close to death quietly sang "Amazing Grace" before drifting back into unconsciousness. I have a beautiful framed copy of that old hymn that I'm gift wrapping for her. It's not a custom around here to give presents on the occasion of a funeral, but I'm breaking with tradition because I think it will really mean something to her. Overcome your "yuck factor" and show a little Grace during your life. You might acquire a priceless friend.

ABORTION AND CHRISTIANITY

Stalwart Sweeties vs. Wanton Wenches

Super Bowl Sunday is coming but the epic battle has already started. The coin has already been tossed, the teams are on the field, and the women are ready to do major battle. On one side stands the Stalwart Sweeties, on the opposing side are the Wanton Wenches. The Sweeties are led by star quarterback Pam Tebow who just happens to be the mother of Heisman winner Gator superstar quarterback Tim Tebow. Notable teammates include Concerned Women for America's CEO Penny Nance; former Alaska Governor Sarah Palin; president of the Susan B. Anthony List and FOX news contributor Marjorie Dannenfelser; and CBS News legal reporter Jan Crawford. The Wenches have President Terry O'Neil of the National Organization of Women as quarterback, along with feminist attorney Gloria Allred and NARAL president Kate Michelman in the backfield. The coaching staff for the Sweeties is from Focus on the Family; for the Wenches it's the Women's Media Center and the Feminist Majority. At stake in this monumental battle is a proposed 30 second commercial for the Super Bowl.

The commercial features the heart-warming story of Tim Tebow's mother when she was pregnant with Tim while working as a missionary in the Philippines. Pam had contracted amoebic dysentery so bad she was in a coma for a while; her doctor informed her the unborn baby could be severely deformed due to placental abruption and advised her to get an abortion. She and her husband prayed about it and decided to carry the baby to term nonetheless, resulting in the birth of Tim Tebow.

The Wenches went on offense first with NOW claiming the ad is a divisive "attack on choice"; an offensive attempt to "dictate morality"; and is "offensive and extraordinarily demeaning." After marching 95 yards down the politically correct football field riding that strategy, the Sweeties countered with a solid goal-line defensive stand. CBS's Jan Crawford stopped the Wenches on the one yard line with this salvo: "…in the middle of the so-called 'family hours' I am covering up my kids faces and singing 'don't watch, don't watch' as some promotional advertisement for an upcoming crime show airs picturing a dead woman, her face smashed on the ground, with a knife in her back. Or an ashen corpse with bulging eyeballs and blood trickling out of its skull… but there's no outrage over these ads that glorify death and violence, that depict women brutalized by crazed psychopaths on the run. No uproar. That's reserved, instead, for ads that 'Celebrate Life' while images of guts and gore continue to seep into our living rooms without protest."

After a missed field goal attempt by the Wenches the Sweeties stormed back on offense with Marjorie Dannenfelser stating "What is the worst case scenario in allowing the ad to air? Women are exposed to an example of sacrifice for the sake of an unborn child. NOW needs to explain where the harm and threat to women and children is here." Penny Nance of CWA related that for over three years she advised the FCC on indecency issues and couldn't remember "one time that NOW ever spoke out about sexually graphic or misogynistic content on CBS … I find it laughable that NOW has a problem with Tim Tebow sharing his own story."

The Wenches on defense have resorted to an all-out ad hominem blitz on Tim's mother Pam – feminist attorney Gloria Allred accusing her of lying. Apparently in 1987 abortion was illegal in the Philippines when she was faced with that decision, thus calling into question her doctor's advice to get an abortion. That sounds a bit fishy for several reasons: first, despite the fact that abortion is still illegal there, underground abortions are nonetheless widely practiced and are rarely prosecuted. The International Planned Parenthood Federation has estimated from 155,000 to 750,000 induced abortions are performed every year; there is a very high maternal mortality rate due to these "back-alley" abortions. Secondly, the Philippine Constitution has a clause allowing legal abortions if the life of the mother is in question. Thirdly, Pam Tebow was an American citizen and could have immediately flown back to the USA to get a legal abortion. I personally think Gloria should be flagged for unsportsmanlike conduct.

Perhaps motivating this whole affair is the fact that Gallop polls indicate, for the first time in a very long time, a slight majority of Americans favor the pro-life position. Marjorie stated that Terry O'Neil of NOW told the *National Journal* that her organization "is struggling and stalled out." The feminists are very well aware they have lost field position and are making an effort to remain relevant. Instead of advocating censorship there is always the mute button. I'm sure I will take some flak for labeling them the Wanton Wenches. Maybe I should have gone with the "Ticked Chicks"? Oh gosh, I'm in trouble now…

Do the Unborn Feel Pain?

Lindsey Tanner, an AP Medical Writer, had an article published in the Wednesday August 24 edition of *The Daily Herald* entitled "Researchers say fetuses feel no pain until late in pregnancy." Her article reported the findings of researchers at the University of California-San Francisco, and those researchers concluded that fetuses cannot feel pain until they are about 28 weeks old.

That conclusion was certainly a surprise to Dr. Jean Wright, who serves as executive director at the Backus Children's Hospital in Savannah, Ga. In an interview with the Web site *CitizenLink*, Dr. Wright stated "Oh please! Anyone who has walked through a neonatal intensive care unit and seen a 25, 26, or 28-weeker knows that's not true. There's a perfect place for studying in-utero pain to the fetus, because we have those babies every single day in our hospitals, essentially on the outside, where we can look at their grimace, see their reaction to pain, and measure their stress hormones. When I look at the 20-week fetus, there are pain receptors that cover the entire body — starting at week six. The nerves have progressed from the head down to the feet; they've connected with the spinal cord; there are little packets of protein that go from one nerve ending to another. When we measure the response to a painful stimulus — either by hormones or other tests we use — all those things are there. Because a baby can't say 'Ouch,' does that not make it pain? I don't think so."

The problem with the research team at the University of California-San Francisco is that they are not neutral on this hot-topic social issue; they have a vested interest in the outcome. Susan Lee was the lead author, and she has been employed by the National Abortion Rights Action League. Many of the physician authors of the study just happen to have ties to the Center for Reproductive Health Research and Policy at that same University, and the center is known for its pro-abortion advocacy. Dr. Elizabeth Drey, one of the authors, is the medical director of an abortion clinic at San Francisco General Hospital. None of those facts were reported in the article that appeared in the Journal of the American Medical Association. That is rather odd for a science-based organization, because the problem of researcher's personal biases filtering into their research efforts is a well-known phenomenon; science organizations that publish research findings usually take pains to ferret out such biases. Most social conservatives have a gut level feeling that if a Pro-Life organization had sent a team of physician members to research this topic, and submitted their research to JAMA, it would have been "deep-sixed" because of a conflict of interest.

Lindsey Tanner's article did quote Dr. Kanwaljeet Anand's objections to this reported finding. Dr. Anand thinks the evidence points towards 20 weeks as being the threshold for feeling pain, and he is not just a "fetal pain researcher" as Tanner states, but rather he is the United States top fetal pain researcher. He was called upon to testify in a partial-birth abortion trial in a New York federal court concerning that 20 week-old threshold.

National Right to Life's Douglas Johnson (legislative director) says that the report's conclusion simply doesn't add up. "It defies common sense to believe that a baby who's been born prematurely can experience pain and needs anesthesia, but a baby a month or five weeks older, who's still in the womb, experiences no pain when her arms or legs are being cut-off. That's what the authors of this paper would have us believe." More than likely the timing of this report's release is a calculated move to sabotage the Unborn-Child Pain Awareness Act, a congressional bill sponsored by Senator Sam Brownback of Kansas and Representative Chris Smith of New Jersey. As the public becomes a little more aware of the details behind this report, it's likely to backfire.

The Big Bang and Abortion

Take a trip into the country away from city lights, and gaze upwards on a cloudless night. The immense number of stars continually fascinates the observer, while inspiring poetic impulse in some, and romantic feelings in others. Then there are those science types who wonder exactly how big the universe really is; are their any boundaries beyond which nothing exists? Is the universe static (unchanging)? Cosmology up to the 20th century had a consensus of scholarly scientific opinion on those questions. Sir Isaac Newton, famous for his discovered laws of gravity and motion, pictured the universe as always in motion and having no boundaries – the concept of infinity, where the galaxies stretch out across the vast expanse of space forever. Infinity applied in reference to time also – there was no beginning or end but rather a universe that operated according to laws of physics that had "always been that way" and "always will be that way."

Much of the 20th century saw a revolution in cosmology, the study of the universe as a whole. In 1929 Edwin Hubble's astronomical observations indicated that galaxies were moving away from each other, and the further out in space they were, the faster they were moving. Corroborating evidence accumulated quickly supporting the expanding universe view. Radio astronomy in 1963 identified quasars as moving away from us at 150,000 miles a second. Reversing that trend back through history leads to the obvious conclusion that at some distant time in the past all the galaxies were together at one time at one place – the startling concept of the beginning of the universe. Scientists today speak of this beginning point as a "singularity" – a tiny little point in space smaller than the period at the end of this sentence. All those galaxies with their tremendous mass were crunched into a point of near zero radius that subsequently exploded into being – the popularly named "Big Bang." Additional evidence for the Big Bang came in 1965 when background heat radiation of just less than three degrees Celsius was discovered throughout the universe, the left-over radiation from the Big Bang. The Steady State view of the Universe has been effectively disproved scientifically. Our universe had a definite, albeit very tiny, beginning.

That phrase about "a tiny point smaller than the period at the end of this sentence" rang a bell in my memory; it has been printed in editorials in newspapers lately. The pro-choice political cadre loves to skewer pro-life rationale by deriding our overweening concern for clumps of cells "no bigger than the period at the end of this sentence." I'm not sure I understand their logic. Some mighty big and important things have come out of small beginnings, such as you, me, our earth, and the whole universe. Does value or worth only increase incrementally as one progresses through time gestationally? Does that trend continue on the other side of birth? Those afflicted with Down's syndrome have made tremendous strides lately, with some becoming movie actors. Are they of less worth than the rest of us normal folk? Do PhD's have more of a right to expensive life extending medical procedures and medication in dire circumstances than the rest of us average people? Should governmental leaders and scientists be moved to the top of the priority list for organ transplants? Is IQ the ultimate test of human value?

The Christian view is that life has inestimable worth no matter who the person is, or how small or insignificant at the start – it's the potential that matters, not the size. I wonder if there was a potential scientist with a cure for cancer among those 40 million abortions over the last four decades. Our looming social security problems are due to an imbalance between a shrinking class of young workers trying to support a much larger elderly class. Take away 40 million abortions, and there would be no shortfall in the social security program. The number of people trying to adopt each year while being frustrated by the expense and red tape is approximately equal to the number of abortions each year – and that's a travesty. The starting point in Christian theology is that all of us are valued highly by God and have equal dignity and worth irregardless of ignoble beginnings. How can one measure the value of potential? That's the point.

Genetic Defects and Abortion

Sometimes the worst of things seem to happen to the best of people. The older you live to be, the more cases you will see like that. At first there is a feeling of horror, then sympathy, then often a profound sense of cosmic injustice. In a perfect world bad things would happen to bad people in hopes they would reform their ways, while good things would happen to good people as a sort of reward system. Our criminal justice system and meritorious reward programs employ those assumptions on opposite sides of the coin.

Health problems violate all "what should happen" rules we sometimes have in our minds. Presently I'm sitting in a hospital room with my wife Susan while she undergoes a series of tests trying to ascertain why she has suffered three mini-strokes in less than one year's time. Strokes are supposed to happen only with 70-plus-year-old smokers who have high blood pressure and have gorged themselves on fried chicken every day. Susan has low cholesterol, no high blood pressure, doesn't smoke, eats healthy — none of the normal risk factors related to strokes. The only risk factor seems to be a family history of strokes on her dad's side, but genetics is no fault of her own.

Especially traumatic are those cases where a mother loses an unborn child, or sometimes a baby brought to term, because of some genetic abnormality. A precious young couple in our church recently lost an unborn baby due to Edward's syndrome (Trisomy 18). Something went wrong in early cell division resulting in three instead of the normal two chromosomes on the 18th spot out of 46 chromosomes. Down's syndrome is a little better known — an extra 21st chromosome. Edward's syndrome is almost always fatal before birth with just a few babies living a few days once they are born. It's a completely random defect with no hereditary causes nor any risk factors the parents could have avoided.

It's especially heartrending when birth defects are involved. There is the "Why did this happen to us" thought along with the horrible feeling, however illogical and unjustified, of "It's our fault we had an unhealthy baby." It's a horrible loss and there's not much one can say to ameliorate the searing pain but to let them know you are praying for them. It's a grieving process that takes a lot of time to partially heal. It's often especially tough in the Christian world because of all those statements heard about the unborn: "God has a plan for everyone from the first day of conception" and "God is creating every part of your being in the womb." In-utero defects vary from missing limbs to part of the spine being outside the body to missing brains. Are we willing to claim that God personally designed those? Around 15-20 percent of pregnancies in our nation result in miscarriages, and about 60 percent of those are spontaneous (natural) abortions. I realize this is an inflammatory question to those in the pro-life community, including me, but is God in the business of natural abortions? I wouldn't think so.

First, theologically speaking, it's a bit of dishonest scholarship to generalize from the particular (God chose John the Baptist from the womb for a specific plan) to the general (God chooses everyone from the womb for specific plans including which schooling, which employer, which friends, which husband, how many kids, etc.). Second, it is presumptuous to lay at the feet of God the blame for every horrible accident and defect when those most often lay properly in the domain of either random chance or Satan's influence. Not that I think Satan is there personally at every miscarriage, but rather that genetic defects and random chromosomal errors entered into the world through sin when Adam and Eve gave Satan the legal right to influence humanity for the worse through accepting his advice — contrary to God's instructions. The Biblical record reveals the increasing imperfections in the human genetic make-up from perfect bodies in the Garden of Eden to progeny living for hundreds of years, gradually decreasing to about seventy years on the average centuries later.

I'm convinced that most birth defects simply happen. We are badly flawed physically, saint and sinner alike. That realization should keep us from blaming God, others, or ourselves for genetic mishaps and perhaps introduce a little more civility in the abortion debate. No, that's undoubtedly wishful thinking.

PROSPERITY THEOLOGY

Scam Artists Part I

Scam artists are swindling big bucks out of church members these days. An Associated Press article entitled "Religion-Related Fraud Getting Worse" provided several egregious examples: $50 million stolen by the JTL ("Just the Lord") investment firm; another $50 million fraudulent real estate scheme perpetrated by Lambert Vander Tuig, a member of Saddleback Church in California; $500,000,000 (yes, half a billion) by Greater Ministries International in Florida who bilked thousands in a "double your money" investment scheme. The unfortunate victims are churches and members alike.

Sometimes it's a Ponzi scheme: they use funds from the newcomers to pay off the prior investors. Real Estate investments are frequent ruses. Occasionally it's that e-mail from Nigeria promising a big return if you will only pay a smaller up-front transaction fee; that particular one suckered the Winkler family in Selmer. It was one of the things they were arguing about the night Mary Winkler shot and killed her Church of Christ minister husband.

A really wacky scheme to hit a few Columbia area churches recently was Dennis Lee's "free electricity" gizmos. All you had to do was invest $275 and shortly Dennis would provide for you an electronic/mechanical gizmo that would generate enough electricity to power your home, leaving you with enough electricity to sell back to the power company. We had some well-meaning church members recently trying to encourage us to invest in this one. Dennis bills himself as a modern day prophet — "God's anointed" — who claims a divinely appointed mission to free Christians from the monopoly of the evil electric companies. He doesn't have the gizmos perfected yet, but he's working on it. This is the same Dennis Lee who defrauded tele-evangelist Pat Robertson out of $150,000 twenty years ago, and the same individual who served two years in prison for consumer fraud.

Why is it that fraud is so easily perpetrated among church members? Is it partly because a certain amount of trust is automatically engendered by someone claiming to be in the Lord's ministry? Could it be that many churches are cash-starved, struggling with big mortgages, and view a promising investment scheme that sounds too good to be true as a God-send and an answer to desperate prayer? Evangelical churches seem especially hard-hit; what predisposes them to this susceptibility? That same AP article noted the increasing acceptance of the so-called "prosperity gospel" as a possible reason for the increased receptivity to the "God wants you wealthy" fraudulent schemes.

I've been involved with evangelical churches all my life and have witnessed firsthand the rise of the "prosperity gospel." As a young man in my early twenties I was taught that philosophy in a small evangelical church that was part of the "Word of Faith" movement. Because I was a bit more gullible back then, it sounded pretty good to me. Study your Bible, claim God's promises of prosperity, and you are guaranteed eventually a happy, fulfilling, and wealthy life. A few years later what I had achieved out of it was a Plymouth Horizon that was falling apart and a job earning minimum wage working for Kresge, the parent company of K-Mart. After wisingup by seriously studying those "wealth promises" in the Bible a little more closely, I left that movement and warned others about the excesses and dangers associated with the "God wants you rich" theology. Since that time I've been blessed with a high-paying job at General Motors with several new vehicles along the way. My life isn't exactly what the prosperity preachers are looking for in the way of an outstanding testimonial.

How is it that good churches and intelligent Christians are increasingly being drawn to the prosperity gospel? There isn't a seminary that falls for it to my knowledge, neither liberal nor conservative. It doesn't filter from "the top down," it bubbles up from the grassroots through popular speakers, books, and tapes. How do they twist the Bible so convincingly from the "Blessed are the poor" of the Beatitudes to the "Blessed are the wealthy?" Having been involved "on the inside" so to speak, it's apropos to reveal how it's accomplished. 'Till next time —

Scam Artists Part II

Scam artists pursuing their fraudulent schemes often find receptive audiences in our churches, as recent news stories have shown. Sometimes the perpetrators overcome initial skepticism by assuring the audience that God's divine plan really is for them to become wealthy — with the stipulation that the wealth is to be used for helping others and spreading the gospel. That philosophy cloaked in Biblical phraseology depends on several common-sense mistakes for its success, and some of them are as follows:

1. Ignore the literary context. Most people are aware how dirty politics takes a statement made by a candidate, lifts it out of the context of their speech and makes it sound like something entirely different. The same can be done with Biblical literature. An example would be *Luke 6:38* — "Give and it shall be given unto you …" The impression left is that the more money you give to Mr. Prosperity Preacher's ministry, the more God will bless you back in various ways with more money. The context, however, reveals that money has nothing to do with the subject being discussed, that being judging others hypocritically. The more critical judgment you give out to others, the more you will receive. Think paragraphs, not individual verses, to follow the flow of thought.

2. Ignore literary writing conventions of the first century. Much is often made of *III John 2:* "Beloved, I wish above all things that thou mayest prosper and be in health..." "Prosper" surely means we should all become rich, right? This epistle was a personal letter written from John to his friend Gaius, and personal letter writing in the first century often followed certain conventions, such as standard greetings or concluding valedictions. Today we follow certain letter-writing conventions such as "Dear Sir" or "Sincerely Yours." First century conventions were a little more elaborate, and John was using a common one to begin his letter to Gaius. The word "prosper" means basically that "all may go well with you" as it is translated in the NIV. To turn a standard greeting into a "get rich" philosophy is simply unethical.

3. Confuse individual promises with corporate covenants. The "Blessings and Curses" for obedience and disobedience in *Deuteronomy 28* are often used as a springboard for the "God wants you rich" philosophy. Those promised blessings were given to the newly formed nation of Israel if the nation as a whole abided by the covenant God had made with them. It did not mean that every individual Israelite would be wealthy if only they were obedient; several examples of poor Israelites can be found in the Old Testament. One of the rules given to Israel was for reapers in the field to leave a little laying in that field for the poor to gather later — the orphans, widows, disabled — those who were poor through no fault of their own.

4. Ignore the effect of "cultural difference" on the definitions of Biblical words. The further removed in geography, time, and customs we are from another culture, the more careful we have to be in the business of translation. "Rich" in ancient agrarian Israelite culture usually meant that a family had a lot of sons, abundant crops, healthy family members, or a lot of sheep and goats. Bear that in mind when reading verses such as *Proverbs 22:4*

— "By humility and the fear of the Lord are riches, and honor, and life." Translating that into luxury cars, millionaire homes, and Lear jets is ignoring cultural differences.

5. Ignore the different motivators used between the two Testaments (Old and New) and the two cultures (ancient Israel and first century Christianity). Promises of physical blessings (good crops, many children, health, etc.) and the converse (curses) were common in the Old Testament as motivations for being obedient to God. The primary motivation in the New Testament is internal — letting the Holy Spirit work through the Christian towards obedience and good works. The Holy Spirit came down on only a select few in the Old Testament, but is promised to every believer in the New Testament. The physical "carrot-and-stick" motivators of the Old Testament have been replaced in the New Testament by the spiritual internal reality of the Holy Spirit indwelling believers. Applying Old Testament verses to New Testament Christians is a theologically risky business.

Cultural differences; literary context; literary writing conventions; individual versus corporate promises; physical versus spiritual motivations; all of these are rarely heard in Sunday morning sermons. Usually it's because the preacher never went to Bible College, or it doesn't seem exciting. The result? Weird philosophies start spreading through our churches unchecked. 'Till next time...

Hard Times for Prosperity Preachers

Every once in a while I read the Sunday edition of *The Tennessean*; last Sunday's paper had an article entitled "Prosperity gospel faces challenge: frugal savers." The author, Bob Smietana, gives a brief description of the prosperity gospel and contrasts it with its alleged opposite – the austerity gospel as taught by popular radio host and author Dave Ramsey with his Financial Peace University, along with Crown Financial Ministries which offers classes in churches on proper budgeting procedures. Bob's article states that these programs are seeing an influx of people who are dissatisfied with the prosperity gospel they had been taught; I was wondering when that would happen, since our economy is so bad right now. Dave Ramsey's program helped me personally to get out of debt aside from the home mortgage and to use credit cards rarely and quickly pay them off. His program is based on some good Biblical principles. To allege, however, that his program is the opposite of the prosperity gospel is not accurate.

The opposite would be the teaching that poverty is a virtue and that money is of an evil influence. Consider the monastics of the 3rd and 4th centuries who lived in voluntary poverty in desert regions living on dry bread and water. Then there is the simplistic wandering poor-preacher model ministering to and identifying with the poor (the Franciscan friars and Dominicans). When I was a child, some preachers in my own church thought that pastors should live in older homes and drive cars at least ten years old "to keep them humble." That type of thinking is not so popular in our materialistic culture today, but the prosperity gospel has many converts here in the U.S. and especially in Africa, where it dominates the religious landscape in poverty stricken nations.

The basic premise behind the prosperity gospel is that God wants to bless Christians materially, so that if you give money to a minister of the gospel, God will somehow bless you back with more money. Old Testament scriptures are often quoted such as the "Blessings for obedience" verses of Deuteronomy chapter 28 and certain proverbs such as "The blessing of the Lord brings wealth…"(Proverbs 10:22). There are many such verses in the Old Testament; one of the main motivating forces behind the Israelites' service to God was the promise of material success in their earthly lives and an avoidance of sickness, military defeat, and poverty if they obeyed the covenant law God had made with them through Moses. It was the reward/punishment system and it was simple. The problem is that it was not a sufficient motivating force to ensure the Israelites' compliance; the Old Testament traces Israel's often and continued rebellion against Moses' law until finally God punishes them with deportation and slavery to both the Assyrians and Babylonians. The first chapter of Isaiah reveals that God was sick of their sacrifices and burnt offerings, their "sacred assemblies," their prayers – the old covenant was disregarded and God expressed his disgust with them throughout Isaiah, Jeremiah, and Ezekiel. Many verses compare Israel to an unfaithful bride that runs off from her husband to find another lover. A new covenant in the future, however, is promised wherein God's law will be "put into their minds and wrote on their hearts" and their sins will be forgiven (Jeremiah 31:31-34).

The New Testament reveals that the new covenant was made through the sacrifice of Jesus Christ and His resurrection, and for those who come to personal belief and salvation through Jesus Christ, sins are forgiven and a new covenantal relationship is established. In the Old Testament the Holy Spirit came down only on a selected few priests, kings, and prophets. The New Testament makes it clear that the Holy Spirit can take up personal residence in the hearts of all who are "born again" (saved, converted, become new believers, etc) and assist them in their motivations to do what is right. That's a huge difference – to have an inward help in wanting to please God instead of relying on external rewards and punishments.

The New Testament is radically different when it comes to the subject of riches. Warnings abound, with too many to list here. Prosperity preachers ignore the warnings and quote their favorite New Testament verse (Luke 6:38) which states "give and it will be given to you." The context is ignored; these verses preceding and following are all about the impropriety of judging others while ignoring your own faults. If you condemn and judge others harshly, then it will be given back to you "pressed down, shaken together, and running over." It is a strict warning about being a judgmental person and has nothing to do with money.

Ignoring literary contexts; relying on an old covenant no longer in force; using a wrong method of external motivation; being judgmental in using wealth as a gauge for God's blessings – it's all stock and trade of the prosperity preachers' vocation (along with a convenient pyramid giving scheme to make themselves wealthy). I think I like Jesus' model prayer a bit better – "give us this day our *daily* bread." Not our "yearly" bread or 20 year's worth of bread, but rather learn to trust the Lord's provisions for you day by day as you work hard and handle your money frugally. That's much better advice, and much more faithful to the Biblical model.

Job Promotion and Prosperity

Every once in a while I compile a mental list of some of the nuttiest, most bizarre, and Biblically distorted assertions that I have heard preached in churches. They say the truth is often stranger than fiction, unfortunately that maxim holds true for concepts sometimes preached from the pulpit. Some of the more oddball ones stem from a simple lack of education on the part of the minister, but it never fails to amaze me how many truly intelligent and well educated folks swallow these assertions hook, line, and sinker without really taking a few moments to think. Here are my latest two candidates for goofy pronouncements from the pulpit in these economically distressing times:

Candidate #1 – "If you are a Christian, pay tithes to your church, keep sin out of your life, and live truly for Jesus Christ, then you will be highly favored in this world. Favor isn't Fair; God will see to it that your résumé will rise to the top of the stack over others more qualified – you will get the job ahead of others. Once you get that job, you will be highly favored by your bosses and get promoted over others who even have more experience than you. Proverbs 14:9 states '…among the righteous there is favor.'"

This is the sure-fire fast-track to career success — what a shame more people don't know about it! Naturally all the top bosses over the years will end up being devout Christians while the lower ranks of employees will inevitably be filled with the unbelievers. But, of course, we have to be careful not to let the unbelieving employees know about this "magic bullet" method of certain career advancement or they might think it awfully discriminatory!

Does being a devout follower of Jesus Christ guarantee me favor over others out there in this world? I remember Jesus making a statement to the effect of "If the world hates you, keep in mind that it hated me first" and "If they persecute me they will persecute you also" (John 15:18-20). Eleven of his twelve disciples suffered martyrdom, and somehow martyrdom just doesn't strike me as having favor. In today's modern culture, believing that there really is a heaven and hell in an afterlife and that Jesus is the only way to heaven is regarded as narrow minded and culturally insensitive, and heaven help you if you really believe the Biblical pronouncements on homosexuality as being an abomination before God! Those beliefs are probably a one-way ticket to job demotion if you make it publicly known in your workplace. I personally know of several devout Christians who lost their jobs because they refused to lie for a boss, falsify a report to make the company look good, or tried to get a long-standing problem solved by going around an incompetent boss (a tactic which often backfires). I know others who, being morally bankrupt, schmoozed, partied, lied, politicked, and slept with the right members of management to get to the top.

Candidate #2 – "If you are a Christian then everything you touch will prosper. Have an idea for a business floating around in your mind? Go for it with gusto because you are guaranteed success in your business endeavors because Psalms 1:3 states '… whatever he does prospers.'"

Well, we all are aware that about 50% of small business owners go belly-up, but what we apparently didn't investigate was the startling fact that there were no dedicated Christians in that 50%!! If you believe that, then I have some land to sell you in Florida. Just forget about doing that tedious market research, comparing your product with competitors in quality and price, estimating overhead and taxes, and seeking business advice from professionals — just jump right into that idea floating around in your head because you are guaranteed success as a Christian! This one is pretty obviously balderdash – no lengthy refutation really needed.

Both these goofy assertions stem more from our American materialistic success-oriented culture than from the Bible. I'm a devout Christian and yes, I am favored **by God**, not necessarily by others. Writing public editorials on Christianity gets me both verbal accolades and menacing glares. If you have a good work ethic, a pleasant personality, stay in school and get a good education, and pursue a career in line with your talents, then most of the time you will prosper. Christians should have those motives and qualities – that is what the Bible assumes in that "prosper" statement. Making it a 100% magic bullet for success without the prior hard work and schooling is foolishness. Funny how some folk always prefer the supernatural spiritual factor over the practical!

Goofy assertions like these only prosper here in America because we are often culturally ignorant. Muslims in other countries who turn to Christ often are kicked out of their families, their tribe, their village – which ensures humiliating disfavor and poverty. They are still favored by God and prosper spiritually, and someday will inherit the riches of heaven as their reward. That's true prosperity. Now, let me see if I can find the deed to that land in Florida for some of y'all out there…

Rewarding Activities Seldom Bring Wealth

I've actually had people here in Columbia ask me if being an editorialist for *The Daily Herald* is my main occupation. They seem genuinely surprised when I inform them I don't make one red cent at it – most local editorial writers for small home-town newspapers write strictly on a voluntary basis. "Oh," they say – "that's all it is!" I've had good-intentioned but misguided relatives urge me to simply quit writing and demand to be compensated for it – to get what I'm worth. Somehow there is an implicit assumption that my worth is forever tied to what my income is. They are also unaware of the terribly stringent budgets that newspaper publishers have to live by these days competing with TV, radio, and the internet as news sources.

Along the same lines I've had people ask me how much I earn teaching basic mathematics to students through Project Learn and chuckle at the shock on their faces – "What? Only $3 an hour? How can they pay so little? Why do you do it?" Explaining how $15 per hour turns into $3 per hour because of the "80% takeaway rule" of unemployment compensation is only a confusing start – it gets much worse. Laid-off GM workers get funds from two separate sources — state unemployment and the corporate

Supplemental Unemployment Benefit (SUB) fund. Both have the "80% takeaway rule" with the exception that unemployment allows me to make $68 per week before that 80% rule takes effect. That means I have to limit myself to 4 hours of work a week ($60) or I will get double-hit and actually lose money.

As an example, if I managed to make $200 a week at a part-time job, then both the state ***and*** GM would take away 80% of that $200 ($160) —- which means that $320 total gets taken away. So for $200 earned I would actually lose $200 - $320 = $(-120). Going to work to lose $120 each week ($480 per month) is simply not high on my list of priorities – it's a powerful disincentive. If you've wondered why laid-off GM workers are not frantically looking for jobs until the SUB fund and unemployment run out, then now you know why. They are not lazy, they just know how to take percentages and subtract.

I find it curious that the things I value most in life do not come attached to a big income figure. Giving of my income each week to my church and expecting nothing back financially isn't good business practice secularly speaking. Some others would rather sit at home and watch the TV preachers. Spending countless hours studying Biblical literature to be a better teacher in a church which does not pay me wouldn't make sense to some folks. Tutoring students in math and losing $3 an hour to gasoline costs and an endless need for dry-erase markers might not seem the bright thing to do. Writing articles for the home town newspaper purely for the joy of writing and expressing a Christ-honoring viewpoint would not be enough motivation for a lot of folks. The almighty dollar and the rat-race to continually earn more takes precedence, and some misguided Christians have even devised a theological defense for their "name it and claim it; blab it and grab it; get it all while you're at it" of "making yourself wealthy is priority #1" philosophy. They sure don't have the attitude of the Apostle Paul in "If we have food and clothing we will be content with that – people who want to get rich fall into temptation and a trap and into many foolish and harmful desires that plunge men into ruin and destruction" (1 Timothy 6:9).

I've never seen a U-haul following a hearse to the cemetery; you simply can't take it with you. I've seen some people who make an astounding income who are absolutely miserable. On the other hand, I have found a genuine satisfaction when a student recently pointed his finger at me and stated "You are the reason I passed my compass math test and am now in the nursing program." It's the same sort of feeling when someone tells me "I appreciated your article so much here lately – thank you." Getting to know people on a personal basis and occasionally help them out in a local church is intrinsically satisfying. Those types of things you just can't put a price tag on, and the One whom I want to please the most is the all-seeing One on the other side of this earthly materialistic sphere of reality. That's the ultimate motivation for me.

No Such Thing as a Christian Beggar?

Economic bad news just seems to come in waves through the media these days. I know some people who quit reading or listening to the news because it's so depressing – a negative avalanche that can seem overwhelming. Everyone knows someone who just lost their job or took a pay/benefits cut; mortgage delinquencies have hit an all time high. First it was Chrysler going bankrupt, now it's GM; watch for a host of auto suppliers to follow suit.

When I talk to Christian friends and relatives who work for GM (as I do), often I hear the following Bible verse quoted: "I have been young, and now am old; yet have I not seen the righteous forsaken, nor his seed begging bread" (Psalms 37:25). It's usually quoted with a certain hint of smugness, as though that verse is the final answer to all economic problems that could beset a Christian believer. It is used as a justification that a true Christian will never actually suffer extreme economic deprivation. It flows along with the popular prosperity belief – as long as you pay your tithes, avoid personal sin, study your Bible, go to church faithfully, and live for Christ then you have an iron-clad guaranty for economic success, and you will certainly never have to be on welfare or seek financial aid from others. Most assuredly you cannot ever be a beggar.

There's a slight problem with that view. David was the author of that particular verse, and as a young man David was in such dire circumstances he had to beg himself. When David was on the run from a murderous King Saul he had to resort to begging some loaves of bread from priest Ahimelech which were ordinarily used in religious ceremonies (1 Samuel 21:3). Many of the Psalms that David later wrote echo those times of sorrow and destitution that we now call "Psalms of Lament." Psalms 37 itself records in verse 16 that at times the wicked are wealthy and the righteous are poor: "Better the little that the righteous have than the wealth of many wicked."

Another problem is that David was indeed used to seeing beggars among God's people in ancient Israel. Those unfortunate Jews who were born with severe birth defects, or who were injured, or who were terminally ill, or widows with no supporting relatives made up a sizeable class of beggars in Israel. They were so common that anyone making the pilgrimage to the Temple in Jerusalem was sure to encounter beggars collecting alms along the way; it was considered a righteous act to give to them. There were so many in the Temple area that laws had to be enacted directing where they could sit to ask alms.

When Jesus met these beggars he did not assume it was because they were not righteous. That was the assumption of the prideful sect of Pharisees. Remember beggar Lazarus lying at the rich man's gate full of sores? It was Lazarus who was the righteous person. Out of all the beggars that Jesus encountered and healed in the Gospels, I can't remember one instance where Jesus condemned them for being in that state of destitution. Being righteous or unrighteous was a separate matter.

When national calamities struck ancient Israel, such as the Assyrian and later Babylonian conquests of Israel and subsequent Jewish deportations, the righteous folks suffered slavery right along with the unrighteous. If God allows a national calamity such as an economic meltdown, to happen right here in the U.S., as many Christians are asserting presently, then all of us will ultimately be affected. Scores of Christian folks have already been affected in this recession. Nehemiah Builders, a locally owned and operated Christian business, just went under financially.

In times of distress we need to have an attitude of helping each other through it all. That was Paul's attitude when he took offerings for the destitute believers back in Jerusalem during his travels. Above all, don't look down your nose at a fellow Christian because he lost his job or home. Don't be surprised if a Christian family comes through your church's food pantry line. Don't be a Pharisee. Also remember that a person on welfare here is considered well-off by many people in other countries. Wealth is a relative concept.

So what did David mean by that statement in Psalm 37:25? Now there's a good case for appropriate Biblical scholarship. Psalms are the poetical release of emotions from the inspired writer up to God expressing their deeply felt joy or sorrow. Treating them like the Ten Commandments from God down to the individual believer reverses that inspiration process for this particular genre of Biblical literature. It's a classic mistake the unlearned make and is a deep subject for another discussion.

What is a Successful Christian Life?

Almost all of the churches I've attended from my youth to middle age had a general idea of what it meant to live a successful Christian life. If one would just accept Jesus Christ as Savior and Lord then everything in their lives would start working out for the better. Bad character habits could be extinguished; prayers would be answered; God would guide you to a future spouse who would be just right for you; one could expect success in schooling and jobs; your needs would be met with a nice house and healthy children; you would be respected in your community; your family would enjoy good health; etc. It's not that we wouldn't ever have to face disappointment or heartache, but generally our lives as a whole surely would be noticeably better than those who never cared to follow Christ. The quality of our lives was supposed to be a witness to those who didn't know Christ – a sign of God's favor upon us. This was especially true for those whom God called into the ministry (preachers, missionaries, evangelists, etc) – their lives would be blessed as they lived their lives in service to others.

For a moment, put yourself in the shoes of Adoniram Judson – the first Protestant American missionary to the country of Burma. In 1813 Judson and his wife Ann left India by ship for Burma. Their very first child died at birth on board that ship.

Arriving in Burma they faced 108 degree heat, malaria, cholera, dysentery, and practically no converts for six years. Their second child, Roger Williams Judson, died at 7 months of age. The First Anglo-Burmese War broke out in 1824; all Westerners were immediately considered spies, so Judson was arrested and dragged out of his home to the infamous death prison of Ava. Knowing that her husband was being tortured, Ann regularly trekked long distances while pregnant through the countryside to visit Burmese authorities and plead for mercy for her husband. The loneliness, sickness, weight loss and stress devastated her health until Ann died 21 months later. Their third child, Maria Elizabeth Buttersworth Judson, died 6 months after her mother at the age of two years old. Three months after Maria's death Judson received word that his father had died 8 months prior. The little church he had built at Rangoon was totally destroyed.

After being released from prison, all the personal tragedy took its toll on Judson. He wrote a letter back to Ann's relatives that stated "My tears flow at the same time over the forsaken grave of my dear love and over the loathsome sepulcher of my own heart." He dug a grave for himself by the hut he was living in and contemplated what his body would look like going through the stages of decomposition. Another letter contained this line: "God is to me the Great Unknown. I believe in him, but I find him not."

Judson's life circumstances just didn't fit the mold of the successful Christian life that I had absorbed from churches throughout most of my life. Most church members would have second-guessed his calling or even his salvation. Many probably would have pitied him for losing most of his faith or losing life's battles to the devil. Judson's life just wouldn't be considered a model for young Christian folks to admire. Their conception was sort of like the old Coca Cola jingle – "Things go better with Coke," only it was "Things go better with Jesus."

If our only standard for success as Christians involves the daily aspects of this present life, such as good health, marriage, kids, schooling, career, home, finances, etc., then I am afraid we have terribly misunderstood the Gospel. Those are the very same things that people all over the world in other religions, or even atheists, desire also. Aren't our motivations as Christians somehow supposed to be different? Shouldn't we be more concerned about what we are working for eternally instead of our comfort and material success in this present world? Didn't Jesus' own disciples face intense persecution and death? Be careful that you don't judge a fellow Christian by their life circumstances, as Paul stated concerning all the troubles that he and other Christians were going through in the 1st century: "If in this life only we have hope in Christ, we are of all men most miserable" (1 Corinthians 15:19).

Judson eventually recovered from his mourning and depression and went on to translate the Bible into the Burmese language, establish 100 churches, and win to Christ over 8,000 Burmese. Due mainly to his influence, Myanmar (Burma) now has the third largest number of Baptist believers in the world, behind the United States and India. He was extremely successful and is indeed a role model for Christians. Please don't turn a judgmental eye towards fellow Christians when they experience heartache, tragedy, or even a loss of faith. Give them time, love, and prayer. Consider eternal values, not temporal values.

Are Prayers for National Prosperity Misguided?

Our economy is sluggishly plodding along with no end in sight to our high unemployment; Obama's stimulus seemed to mostly stimulate banks and Wall Street to continue their egregious behavior such as big bonuses for executives and further speculative monetary risk taking. Many folks are losing their faith in our government's ability to end this recession. Some claim it is already a depression, others see a genuine depression right around the corner. Since we have an interconnected global economy, a financial meltdown in one of the troubled European nations could easily trigger another Great Depression. I'm sure there are many Christians praying that God will prevent such an occurrence. Others pray for a spiritual revival here in America so that God can bless our nation once again. I'm going to suggest something counterintuitive, perhaps quite controversial: an economic depression could actually lead to, or occur concomitantly with, a spiritual revival here in America.

Severe recessions and depressions are nothing new in our relatively short history as a nation. Around 1815 we had a depression that lasted about six years. In the Panic of 1819 there were widespread foreclosures, bank failures, collapsed real estate prices, and a slump in agriculture and manufacturing. During that same timeframe up until the early 1830's, America was experiencing the "Second Great Awakening" – a great spiritual revival that turned many Americans back to Christianity via revival meetings resulting in many personal salvations nationwide. Famous preachers included Charles Finney, Alexander Campbell, Lyman Beecher, James Taylor, and others. That spiritual awakening resulted in the emergence of the Restorationist movement, the Holiness movement, the Churches of Christ, the Disciples of Christ, and greatly strengthened the Methodists and Baptists.

The Panic of 1857 lasted about 1 year and 6 months. The failure of Ohio Life Insurance and Trust Company resulted in a run on the banks – over 5,000 banks failed. Coincidently it was in 1857 that the Prayer Meeting revivals were started in urban areas by Finney, Beecher, and Barnes. It quickly became a big-city phenomenon for two full years until about 1859.

The Panic of 1873 was so severe that the New York Stock Exchange was down for ten days. Unemployment was over 14% and about 18,000 businesses failed over two years. The resulting Long Depression lasted about 5 years and 5 months. Just coincidently the Third Great Awakening (or Layman's Revival) was going on at the same time; the most famous preacher was Dwight L. Moody. It was Moody's two year tour of the British Isles from 1873 to 1875 and being invited to preach in the Hippodrome in London that earned him a national reputation here in America. Other notable preachers who came to prominence were William Booth of the Salvation Army, Charles Spurgeon, and Ira D. Sankey. It was estimated that there were around 50,000 Christian conversions weekly.

The Panic of 1907 to 1911 witnessed a series of bank and trust failures; the stock market crashed to half of its value. In 1929 the Great Depression began; economic production dropped 50% and the unemployment rate hovered around 25%. Coincidently, it was in 1906 that the Final Great Awakening had its most observable beginnings – the Pentecostal movement with its distinctive emphasis on Holy Spirit baptism had begun in the Asuza Street revival in Los Angeles. That movement exploded in numbers in the following years, resulting in the formation of the Assemblies of God, the Church of God, the Church of God in Christ, the Church of God of Prophecy, and the Foursquare Gospel churches. Other groups that grew noticeably during this timeframe were the Seventh Day Adventists and a good number of independent churches that adhered to the dispensationalism of the Darbyites and the Scofield Bible. These groups especially thrived in their appeal to those who felt alienated or disinherited from society, and there were plenty of folks like that during the Great Depression years.

Statistically speaking correlation does not necessarily imply causation. Skeptics will argue that when people lose all faith in government, banks, and businesses during depressions, they may turn to God as a last resort. As a devout Christian I believe God can often allow very difficult circumstances to happen to inspire great revivals right when people need them the most and are the most receptive. That's what happened with the nation of Israel in the Old Testament during the time of the Judges. Israel would descend into unbelief and idolatry during times of prosperity, and then return to God in times of national tragedy. Praying for national prosperity for America in a materialistic, God-forgetting post-Christian era might not be the wisest option. If God in his sovereignty decides to allow another Great Depression, there could well be a silver lining.

BIBLICAL INTERPRETATION

Red Letter Christians

The talking-points bulletins are being mailed to members and the fundraising is in full swing. Religion gurus have been hired and groomed for public appearances, and faith talk is conscientiously inserted into every public speech. Political topics are referenced to chapter and verse while websites are beefed-up to answer the critics. All of this is done, of course, in hopes of influencing the American public of Christian persuasion to vote for the presidential candidate of their choice next election. Who is this group? The "Religious Right"? Why no, it is the "Red Letter Christians."

Say what? Who are the "Red Letter Christians"? They are a group of progressive religious leaders who, in the words of one of their founders, Tony Campolo, are "increasingly disturbed by the alliance between evangelical Christians and the Republican Party." Tony and the other co-founder, Jim Wallis of *Sojourners* magazine, are apparently upset that the religious right repeatedly emphasizes the conservative position on abortion and homosexual rights and garners much of the evangelical vote in doing so – to the tune of 83% voting Republican in the last presidential election. While claiming to be non-partisan and beholden to neither the Democratic nor the Republican Party, their stated points of political interest sounds like, well, bulleted talking points on some Democratic candidate's platform.

Two of their major concerns are the environment and eliminating poverty, while lambasting the gay-bashing, anti-feminism, pro-war, pro-gun, and Religious Right politics. They are against capital punishment, refuse to condemn abortion, and express outrage at our country's militarism. They think that the Religious Right's stand against gay marriage is discrimination due to sexual orientation. A disdain for the excesses of capitalism and American militarism along with a sympathy for political systems that redistribute wealth (such as socialism) lead directly to their stated positions on eliminating poverty and criticism of the American military. All of their political issues can be justified theologically, so they say, directly from Jesus' words in the Bible – the words printed in red ink in many New Testaments.

In order to buttress support for their left-leaning political positions from the Bible, they have formed the Red Letter Christians organization. They believe Jesus' words, especially the Sermon on the Mount, support their positions and attempt to influence Democratic congressmen on the finer points of including such "God talk" in their campaign speeches. They give greater authority to Jesus' words and less to the black letters – it's a clever way to avoid all those Old Testament verses and Apostle Paul's teachings that directly contradict their political positions.

Personally I'm not so sure they have researched the "Red Letters" as minutely as they lay claim to have done. I wonder how Jesus' instructions to His disciples to sell their coats if they have to in order to purchase a sword fits in with their gun-control position? (Luke 22:36). Hmmm. Wasn't it Jesus himself who stated in Luke 11:21 that a "strong man, fully armed, guards his own house, his possessions are safe"?

Jesus was indeed extremely concerned about helping the poor, and doing so is one of the hallmarks of true Christianity. Does that translate directly, however, into massive government programs to rob middleclass Peter and upper class John to pay lower class Paul? Regarding the total elimination of poverty, wasn't it Jesus Himself who stated that "the poor you will always have with you"? (John 12:8). The occasion for that statement was His disciples shock at Mary pouring a whole bottle of perfume on Jesus' head and feet – so expensive that it cost about a full year's wages. Their objection sounds like something coming directly out of a liberal's mouth: "Why wasn't this perfume sold and given to the poor?" (Matthew 26:8, John 12:5).

The promotion of world peace is indeed a worthy goal, but does that translate directly into an anti-war, anti-military stance towards our own country's military? Wasn't it Jesus Himself who gave that Roman Centurion the ultimate compliment "I have not found anyone in Israel with such great faith" (Matthew 8:10) without once denigrating his occupation? It was Jesus Himself who predicted that there would be "wars and rumors of wars" along with "nation will rise against nation" right up until the end times.

Perhaps they should change their name to the "Red Letter Christians Asterisk" (RLC*). The asterisk stands for all those red letter verses that have been put on the banned list – surely they were inserted by some prejudiced monk in the Scriptural transcribing business. Once you let the camel's nose of "cultural bias" into the Red Letter interpretation tent you never know where it will stop. Remember the "Jesus Seminar" where liberal theologians could only agree on one Red Letter verse that was truly genuine? They must be the "One Verse Christians." I personally think it's all God's Word.

Automatic Writing?

The preacher glares down at the congregation and with a flushed face and thundering voice proclaims, while waving the Bible over his head, "This is what the Word of God states: God said it and I believe it – that settles it!" I've seen that scenario happen a few times in my life; if you have attended conservative churches, I'll bet you have also. Often it doesn't matter which book of the Bible or which particular verses they are referring to, just whatever Scriptures they have in mind at the moment is "Word of God" directly from God to you. That was the type of preaching I was raised under – where the entire Bible from cover to cover was asserted to be the very words of God directly to the reader. About thirty years ago the subject became sort of a litmus test as to whether one was a conservative or liberal Christian. Liberals were those people who believed the Bible was simply a collection of culturally influenced and redacted sayings and hero myths that wasn't to be taken literally. They would say the Bible "contained" the words of God rather than "was" the word of God.

Over two decades ago I remember asking my very conservative pastor what he thought about the controversy. He replied with "Do you know that the Bible states 'There is no God'?" I was stunned for a second until I recalled that verse in Psalms 14:1

that in context read "The fool has said in his heart 'There is no God.'" My pastor asked me if "There is no God" were the words of God or the words of a fool, to which I meekly replied "a fool." His reply caught me off-guard and prompted me towards a little deeper Biblical reflection. For those agnostics or atheists out there, I intend no disrespect for your character by that verse; our modern usage of the word "fool" is quite different than how the psalmist David used it. Today we think of it in intellectually disparaging terms – like a stupid person or someone with a low IQ. Old Testament wisdom literature uses it to mean someone who ignores spiritual reality and God's influence in their lives. In that sense a mentally challenged person who loves God and serves Him is "wise" while a university professor who purposely ignores God is the "fool."

The principle not to be ignored here is that the Bible records words that have been spoken by evil men, enemies of God, uneducated and unwise individuals, corrupt kings, common criminals, demons, and the Devil himself. Before we assert "This is the Word of God," we had better investigate to see who is doing the talking. A good example is the Book of Job. The first three chapters describes the horrible tragedy that befell Job; the next 34 chapters contain some very poetical and elegant arguments by Job's three friends that all imply it was Job's fault in some way; the last four chapters reveal God's thoughts on the situation – and God was very displeased with the uncompassionate and judgmental attitudes of Job's friends. In other words fully 34 out of 41 chapters are chock full of faulty theology – the whole point of Job's story is that we shouldn't automatically assume someone in extremely difficult circumstances has brought it on themselves necessarily.

Then there are those "Oh, by the way" statements of Paul in the New Testament that caught my attention. There are the personal "hellos" sent to lists of named friends at the end of several books; the "Wow, look how large these alphabet letters are that I am writing!" comment in Galatians 6:11; the "I am going to spend the winter in Nicopolis" of Titus 2:12; and the "oops, please bring the coat I left behind at Troas when you come" of 2 Timothy 4:13. These are personal comments from the mind of Paul just like the ones that you and I have every day. On one occasion Paul was very careful to distinguish between the very words of the Lord on the subject of marrying as opposed to his own personal advice (1 Corinthians 7:10, 12). My conclusion is that the Biblical writers were not in a trance with their hand picking up a quill and writing all by itself God's words — sort of like the automatic writing of the psychics. Rather they wrote Scripture as they were influenced by the Holy Spirit while at the same time their minds played an active role in the writing process. It was cooperation between the human and the divine.

Hopefully that view doesn't classify me as one of those hated liberals — I still believe God has spoken through the accurate record and closed canon of the Bible, and it's our responsibility to believe and obey. I like that "cooperation" idea — after all we teach Christians today to let the Holy Spirit lead and guide them in their lives. Jesus was the ultimate and unique example — both fully God and fully man. Hmmmm ... something to think about.

Implications of the Dead Sea Scrolls

Recently *The Daily Herald* ran an article about the Dead Sea scroll exhibit down in Mobile, Alabama that piqued my interest. Reading about the 2000+ year old scrolls in my studies of Biblical literature is not the same as laying my eyes on them, and having a chance to see them here in the U.S. without going to Israel is that once-in-a-lifetime opportunity, so my wife and I made the trip to Mobile.

It takes a miracle of preservation to have ancient vellum (leather-based parchment) or Egyptian papyri survive for that long of a period of time, and that miracle is in the extremely dry climate of the Dead Sea area of Israel. The unknown individuals who placed them in clay jars in the caves there (probably of the Essenes sect) undoubtedly knew that – it was their intention to preserve their writings from the invading Romans far into the future. Most of the fragments were very dark from aging, so dark that the black Hebrew letters were hard to see; scholars used infrared light to help decipher much of the lettering. The room was intentionally very dim; bright lights illuminating the display would have hastened the deterioration of these extremely fragile documents. There were portions, however, that were light enough to clearly see the Hebrew letters. I was surprised at the skill of the scribes – the letters were not thick or crudely drawn; they were extremely fine and drawn with exacting precision, much like a modern calligrapher would do with a very-fine point calligraphy pen. Also interesting were the coins found there, and the other artifacts made out of wood or leather that normally don't survive the centuries – the wooden bowls, leather cords and covers for the scrolls, and a tiny wooden hair-comb with a coarse side for general grooming and a fine side for lice removal.

The Dead Sea scrolls are not simply dry dusty history only relevant to ancient language scholars; they have major implications concerning the reliability of our present Biblical text that has been copied innumerable times throughout the centuries, which impacts theological beliefs. Previously our oldest Old Testament was the Alepps Codex and the Saint Petersburg Codex which only dated to rather recent 8th to 9th centuries A.D. (A humorous sidelight was that all dates in the museum were "B.C.E." and "C.E." –Before Common Era and after Common Era. The PC police have had their say in museums, asserting that "B.C." and "A.D." are culturally offensive. I guess the easily-offended cultures are not supposed to reflect on what that year "0" means in the "Common Era" terminology.) The problem is that the Old Testament was written in its various books at different times going all the way back to 23 centuries earlier. How accurate were those generations of copyists?

A by-product of the Age of the Enlightenment and accompanying Rationalism was a revolution in theology, resulting in the Biblical Criticism method that began in Germany in the mid 19th century and which spread throughout the scholarly world. Various scholars argued that Israel's religion had evolved from a primitive polytheistic religion, which would be reflected in their religious documents, if much older ones could only be found. Accounts of miracles were viewed with suspicion, as though they were spurious accretions to the text only inserted to bolster a particular Jewish leader's credibility – the Bible needed to be "demythologized." It was assumed that scribes from differing sects of Judaism throughout the centuries would have gradually changed parts of the text through their editing in support of their parochial interpretations. Supposedly prophetic verses that found their fulfillment in events of history would have been inserted after the fact. Much of Protestant theological study in the 20th century was trying to ascertain what genuine parts of scripture existed that could actually be trusted.

When that young Bedouin shepherd searching for his lost goat threw that rock into a cave in 1947 and heard breaking pottery, he unwittingly threw a time-delayed bomb into the heart of entrenched liberal Biblical criticism methodology of Protestant theological institutions. Well-preserved sections of scripture from every Old Testament book except Esther were found dating back a thousand years earlier than our oldest manuscripts. Fifty years of scholarly research has found that aside from a few spelling changes and minor variations, they are "almost identical" and "virtually unchanged" from out present Old Testament text (words in parentheses were taken verbatim from a plaque in the museum). The preservation and transmission of our scriptures throughout the centuries has been spectacularly successful; those scribes obviously took their occupation very seriously. The Dead Sea Scrolls provide primary evidence that the "hard left turn" in theological institutions over the last 150 years has been a "wrong turn." God promised to preserve his word to all generations in scripture, and very fragile manuscripts are verifying that point. It's time to make a U-turn.

The Gnostics versus Scriptural Authority

I'm just getting ready to submit for publication my new biography on Abraham Lincoln. I'm going to reveal some new startling details not commonly known. John Wilkes Booth was actually a close secret friend of Lincoln's. Booth actually knew President Lincoln better than any of his relatives or government officials he worked with every day. Completely unknown to the general public, Lincoln had a severe personal phobia about his looks and physical body. He actually wanted to be liberated from his body, and so sought the assistance of his good secret friend Booth to assassinate him in Ford's Theater. John Wilkes Booth is therefore actually the hero rather than the villain history portrays him as being.

What's the source and credibility of this radical information, you ask? Why it's a "secret" knowledge possessed by only a select few worthy individuals such as myself — you must simply take my word for it. Can you imagine the reaction academic elites and the mainstream media would have if I really were attempting such foolishness? Who am I to claim such intimate radical knowledge approximately 150 yeas after the fact? I'm basing my illogical facts on a supposed secret knowledge available only to a select worthy few? Publishers would rightly reject my biography and I would justly be classified as another loony nut case. Simply another nutty conspiracy theory, and not a good one at that. As strange as my concocted story sounds, that is precisely the logic that secular academic elites are employing here recently in a major news story, and mainstream media are playing it up big.

"A new gospel has been unveiled by the National Geographic Society" trumpets NPR on its Day to Day program. "Was Judas innocent?" asks the National Geographic in its article. MSNBC declares that the "controversial manuscript is authenticated as early Christian writing." An article in *The New York Times* stated, "The text gives new insights into the relationship of Jesus and the disciple who betrayed him." Overseas in London *The Guardian* dramatically asks — "A seismic moment for the Christian church?" No one seems to question the validity of a manuscript written about 150 years after the fact that flatly contradicts all other numerous manuscripts about Jesus' life that were scrutinized, compared, and laboriously hand copied by legions of punctilious scribes.

This Gospel of Judas was written by a sect called the Gnostics — from the Greek word "gnosis" meaning "knowledge." They thought they had a secret knowledge revealed only to them, and spiritual salvation was only allowed to those highly favored individuals who possessed this secret knowledge—like themselves. Please pardon the frank language, but they were a weird bunch of people. They taught that matter was evil. The chair you are sitting on — evil. The food you eat — evil. Your physical body — evil. The only thing "good" was of a spiritual nature. Some refused to bathe, not wanting contact with "evil" water! Others saw nothing wrong with adultery, prostitution, group sex, etc. because the body was evil anyway. It was the Gnostics who concocted the theory that Jesus actually never had an evil physical body, or if he did, he wanted to be rid of it as soon as possible. Thus their Gospel of

Judas portrays the hero Judas assisting his master by betrayal so that Jesus could get rid of his degrading physical flesh. They denied the reality of Jesus' physical resurrection on that basis.

Why do the secular media assign such importance to such an obviously biased, not to mention illogical, theory from a sect with a philosophical ax to grind —150 years after the fact? Why do they fall so easily for the accusation that the Gnostics were the true early Christians, while established Christianity was supposedly busy trying to cover-up the real facts? I have a conspiracy theory for that — perhaps a little more credible. The election of George W. Bush was made possible in part by the resurgence of conservative value voters, and liberals realize correctly that many conservatives hold a view of scripture as sacred and authoritative. Anything that questions the validity of scripture with scholarly overtones is right up their alley. They would agree with the Gnostics about Jesus' physical resurrection nonsense. They would prefer celebrating this coming Easter Sunday morning by decorating Easter eggs and eating chocolate Easter bunnies. Nothing wrong with that, but I will be in church celebrating the real reason. It's Resurrection Sunday.

KJV Only?

Newspapers occasionally print a recent best-seller list of books, which sometimes is subdivided into paperback/hardcover or fiction/non-fiction categories. There is one particular book that is always intentionally omitted from that list – the Bible. No matter which category one would assign it to, the Bible would always be at the top of the list; it outsells everything else, and hence its omission. Bibles come in a bewildering variety of translations, from the venerable old King James Version to more recent translations such as the New International Version. Bible translation is a lot of linguistic science plus a little art – there are a few ancient words that we are still uncertain as to their exact meanings. It is almost never the case that a Hebrew or Greek word translates directly into an equivalent modern English word. There are pools of meaning for ancient words, pools of meaning for modern words, and the different pools usually overlap but don't precisely coincide. Consider the English word "board" – do you think you know what it means? It's actually impossible to know what that word means unless you already know what the person is talking about – a piece of wood, room and board, board a ship, a deacon board, etc. Ancient words are similar; they often have closely related differing shades of meaning or entirely different meanings altogether.

Some well-intentioned but misinformed people have argued that the King James Version is the only truly accurate or inspired translation, with all the others being inferior. Such a viewpoint betrays a lack of understanding about the origin of the KJV itself. There were several different translations before the KJV came out in 1611. The Geneva and Bishop's Bibles were well accepted, and when the KJV was first published, a lot of people didn't see the need for a new translation. That wasn't the only problem. The 1611 KJV was found to have quite a few translation errors, and it was constantly being corrected in subsequent years- 1612, 1613, 1616,1629, 1638,1660, 1683,1727, 1762, 1769, and 1873 to be precise. There were some groups of people who actually advocated banning the KJV because of the translation errors. The 1613 edition was popularly known as the "Wicked Bible" because the 7th Commandment left out the word "not" – it actually stated "Thou shalt commit adultery"!

The KJV translators themselves stated that it was not a perfect translation; they provided alternate renderings in their margins, and stated that "a variety of translation is profitable for finding out the sense of the Scriptures." They criticized their own original work by subsequent corrections in later editions. To require everyone to use the KJV exclusively is quite unfair to those who are not very proficient with Middle English – it's a lot like reading Shakespeare in the original edition. Scientific testing on "readability" has found the following grade-levels for these translations: KJV – 12th, NASB – 11th, RSV – 10th, TLB – 8th, NKJV – 8th, and the NIV – 7th. Just try explaining to a barely-literate person what such KJV phrases such as these mean: "ouches of gold," "collops of fat," "naughty figs," "hole's mouth," "clouted upon their feet," and "fetched a compass." The last one is my favorite; it simple means "to turn around."

I will personally follow the KJV translator's advice and use several different translations in my studies. I enjoy the NIV for readability and tracing the general flow of thought through paragraphs, while the KJV is excellent for word studies – every word is numbered and cross-referenced in many Hebrew and Greek dictionaries. Regardless of translation, it would be a shame for anyone not to read it through in its entirety. How can a person be well read if he has never read the best seller of all time?

INTERDENOMINATIONAL COOPERATION – IMPOSSIBLE?

The Value of Differing Denominations

A newcomer to American style democracy can well be overwhelmed by the multiplicity of differing political views. There are the few major divisions, such as Republican, Democrat, Independent, Libertarian, and a few others, but there are also many more divisions within these main parties. The terminology used in news reporting alone is enough to impress one of that fact: conservative, liberal, centrist, dove, hawk, secularist, traditionalist, environmentalist, feminist, social program advocates, private sector advocates, isolationists, internationalists, evolving constitutionalists, original intent constitutionalists, capitalists, socialists, et cetera. Those are off the top of my head, and I'm sure you can think of more. All political factions are supremely confident in the rightness of their viewpoints, and public debate can be intense and even spiteful during an election year. I've heard a co-worker argue that the Democratic Party should be the only party – all the other ones are spurious and should simply fade away! Other political parties likewise have their blinder-wearing zealots. I think the Founding Fathers of our country realized that no one individual or party would ever have an absolute monopoly on all knowledge and truth, and wisely constructed a constitutional system replete with checks and balances, and welcomed multi-party political participation.

A third-world dictator might well look at all our political diversity and conclude "What a mess." Candidates are constantly arguing; representatives are voted in and right back out; the direction of national policy changes with each new President; critics ridicule governmental leaders publicly; and legislation often gets bogged-down through congressional gridlock. A tyrant would think such a system to be horribly inefficient, and would ask, "Which political faction are the people supposed to believe in? That system can't possibly be right." Our reply would be that through the messy filter of often rancorous public debate and arduously difficult consensus-making, the best and most practical policies eventually emerge. Our Founding Father's hope was that the fundamental core values of our democracy would eventually prevail in fostering good governmental legislation in this Republic. The inarguable bedrock core truth of politics is that a nation needs a civil government and a strong military, the lack of which results in anarchy or subjugation. It's just the "how" and "extent" that citizens differ on.

Much the same conceptual framework can be found in modern Christianity. There are several hundred different denominations in these United States alone, and each one is absolutely sure they have cornered the market on Biblical doctrine. Skeptics assaulting Christian belief because of the multiplicity of denominations are much like that third world dictator who cannot see the value of diversity. The differing minor doctrines representing the "how" and "extent" that Christians see differently all rest upon the bedrock of core truths that denominational founders penned into their creeds. There are commonalities in those creeds that transcend denominational boundaries, and the differing opinions and scholarly debate in religious circles only points towards the critical importance of those core truths. Psychologically well-adjusted people don't normally argue with strangers over trivial or inconsequential things – they argue over things they consider to be so foundational as to be ultimately defining of their most treasured values. If it isn't important, people don't waste their time and efforts debating it.

The existence of hundreds of denominations used to bother me as a young man, but not anymore. Some wonderful nuggets of Christian truth have come my way from scholars in denominations other than my own. Actually, there are only two types of denominations that worry me now: the liberal extremists who really don't believe the scriptures or Jesus' deity anymore, and the radically myopic conservatives who think their little group is the only one going to heaven. The former espouses the "I'm OK, you're OK" philosophy; the latter thinks everyone outside their own four walls is definitely "Not OK" – they are the ones wearing blinders hoping all the others will slowly fade-away. I'm afraid that on Judgment Day the former will definitely be "Not OK," while the latter will discover to their amazement they are not alone in heaven. Between these unfortunate extremes exists the bulk of authentic Christianity.

It's usually ignorance that demands absolute uniformity. True Biblical unity overlooks fallible human perceptions and enables us to work harmoniously in service to the Infallible One. It will only be in his tender care on the other side of this fleshly realm that all denominations will effortlessly coalesce into one. Until that time we will have to learn the art of disagreeing agreeably on the finer points of our faith, and view our denominational diversity as human expressions of foundational Christian truth. Whether in the political or religious realm, there is nothing wrong with courteous civil debate. Through all of the human folly of arguing, posturing, thrust and parry, commend and condemn –just remember that good government is critically necessary and so is the Christ. That's the foundational bedrock.

A Cooperative Model

In case you haven't heard, the big church news here lately is how the Northside Baptist Church, Highland Church of Christ, and St. Peter's Episcopal Church joined together in helping the Bethel African Methodist Episcopal Church put a new roof on their sanctuary. Running a close second to that were several Pentecostal churches in the Columbia area who took up a joint love offering to help Scribner's Mill Church of Christ out in Culleoka for the purpose of recovering from recent flood damage. Then there was the absolutely frivolous lawsuit brought against Zion Christian Academy, against which they simply couldn't afford the attorney fees to defend themselves. After hearing a few basic details concerning the "molehill into a mountain" issue, officials from Columbia Academy, Sacred Heart School, Agathos School of Columbia, and Seventh Day Adventist School took that information back to their respective churches. The pastor's councils in those churches enlisted aid from other Church of Christ, Baptist, Catholic, and Seventh Day Adventist churches and those attorney fees were paid for. The lawsuit is expected to be determined in Zion Christian Academy's favor very shortly with all attorney fees reimbursed to the defendant, which will then be returned to all the participating churches.

"Wait a minute," you might be thinking – "why haven't I heard anything about this in the news lately? Besides that it is impossible – churches from different denominations simply don't cooperate together like that." You would be both right and wrong. Of course that first paragraph was entirely fictional – no new roof for Bethel A.M.E.; no flood damage to Scribner's Mill; no lawsuit against Zion Christian Academy. But different churches can indeed cooperate together like that – and already are as a matter of fact. All you have to do is change the name of the locality and the churches in the first paragraph.

When the Del Centro First Baptist Church ran out of money for the second story of their church building, the non-denominational Vision of the Future Church ten blocks away helped finance it. When an Anglican church was looking at ending its Sunday School program because of a lack of qualified teachers in 2008, pastor Norberto Saracco's Pentecostal church had four volunteers to fill in for those vacant positions temporarily in 2009, carrying on that church's curriculum to save their Sunday School program. When a small Pentecostal church had a lawsuit filed against them over a property dispute, pastor Saracco sent out an Email to the "Council of Pastors" in his city – and pastors from many different denominations responded with financial help to resolve that dispute, saving the church. Another lawsuit filed against a Christian school resulted in that "Pastor's Council" raising money to pay for teacher's salaries and the tax debt until the lawsuit was won and the school was back on its feet. Where did these things happen? The country is Argentina and the city is Buenos Aires. These examples and more are detailed in Jeremy Weber's article "Something Better Than Revival" in the June 25, 2010 issue of *Christianity Today*.

That impressive model of interdenominational cooperation didn't happen by accident. It arose from humble beginnings of five local pastors meeting together for the purpose of creating friendships between pastors. The Buenos Aires Council of Pastors was born and many other pastors became interested – to the point currently of around 180 pastors representing some 150 different churches participating. The goal was not attempting to harmonize doctrine – that's an impossible task. The goal was to recognize that their own church was not the only church in town and that finding worthwhile projects to work together on multiplied the success ratio while engendering some good fellowship along the way. That model became a great success and spread beyond Buenos Aires – such as in the town of Neuquén. Pastors from different churches there pooled money to build Christian radio stations, while others formed a Christian HMO that provides basic medical services at very low fees for the poor.

Could that model ever become a reality in the United States or even here in Columbia? Here pastors often don't even know each other, although their churches might be on the same street. A few churches here believe that all other denominations are non-Christian because they have varying beliefs about communion, the mode of water baptism, rules concerning divorce, supernatural gifts for today, eternal security, or worship styles. A common joke is that these isolationist churches will be given a special sound-insulated room in heaven so that they will not be horrified to learn of the presence of other church members who have made it there likewise.

It all depends on what constitutes a Christian. In Buenos Aires the common standards were basic beliefs such as the Trinity, forgiveness of sins through Jesus' death on the cross, and Jesus' future second coming to earth – sort of the "Billy Graham" message. All the other issues were left to the individual churches. Cooperating on common projects provided a powerful witness of love to outsider non-Christians, and made successes possible that were clearly impossible for an individual church. The "Habitat for Humanity" program is an excellent example in this regard. It's a model to think about – maybe even emulate?

Compassion is Not Political

There my wife and I stood in the middle of a gutted out house on East Ninth Street in a neighborhood that most folks who don't live there avoid like the plague. Decade's old dust was raining down from interior deconstruction while about thirty volunteers scurried about ripping down rotted wood and scooping up wheelbarrows full of debris. Aubrey Flagg, geography professor at Columbia Community College, and I were engaged in a polite conversation. Aubrey complimented me on expressing myself well in my editorials, while I respected the deep passion he has for those college kids he teaches. Aubrey had blood running down his arm from nail stab wounds while I had a blood running down my skinned shin and a surgically repaired lower back that was barking at me. The irony of it all slowly dawned on me.

Most white folks in Columbia wouldn't want to be stuck in the middle of a black neighborhood on the east side for any reason whatsoever. It's an area noted for drug sales and occasional gang activity. A police officer that attends my church rolled by and asked me through his open window if everything was going well and did we need any help? A few seconds after talking with him, a black fellow drove by and yelled at me – "Yo, I see they all up in yo bidness too!!" My wife and I had a good laugh about that. We see a police car and have a warm feeling about it; many in the black community see that same police car and have that "here they come down on us again" feeling. Our little volunteer group was there working on the King family home as part of Project Compassion. We really got an emotional boost when People Helping People announced they were giving us $10,000 to help with all the repair work in this humanitarian endeavor.

Aubrey would be classified as progressive or liberal politically while I would be considered conservative. We are both Christians and what brought us together was a common passion – a heart of compassion for helping out some folks who couldn't help themselves – part of Jesus' mission 2000 years ago. We could work together in a not-so-safe environment and carry on a very courteous conversation despite political differences because we shared that same passion. I only wish our society as whole could have that same common courtesy with each other, instead we seem to be getting more polarized and verbally offensive – especially right before election time.

I've started taking the political fliers out of my mailbox and transporting them directly to the trash receptacle. I've seen Democrats mischaracterize their Republican opponents by resorting to digging up "facts" that occurred decades prior and then engage in character assassination by using those "facts" out of context. I've seen a Republican lady running for Representative who was nice enough to knock on my door and talk to me who then proceeded to mischaracterize her Democratic challenger on the immigration issue by quoting one "debatable" statement about immigrants while ignoring the many statements he made that coincided with her own view. I'm sure they would argue that negative campaigning works so those lies-by-omission are justified. I don't think so, and neither do I believe the All-Knowing One whom I so feebly attempt to serve would think so either.

Striving for Christian Unity

Striving for unity in Christianity is not an easy task, even though it is commanded in the New Testament. When one looks at the proliferation of different Christian denominations in our country (much more world wide) it seems to be a downright impossible mission. Mention the very word ecumenical and some pastors and lay people will become instantly defensive, as though to say "No one is going to change anything about what I believe just to be friendly with other churches!" It sometimes comes to a really embarrassing head, as when Billy Graham was in Nashville a few years ago for one of his crusades at the Titans football stadium. I really enjoyed hearing him in person but was shocked by members of a certain denomination picketing the event outside with signs condemning Billy Graham for preaching a false gospel. Apparently their main issue was that Billy wasn't baptizing them in water right there in the stadium. Pretty much the same thing happened with the Promise Keepers meetings for Christian men in football stadiums – it wasn't long before they were taking flak from certain churches. Many of the Pentecostal churches have classified themselves as Full Gospel churches, a term which implies that all the other churches only possess a partial Gospel! I remember reading with fascination when David Du Plessis, a Pentecostal scholar, went to the Vatican simply to share his Biblical views and Christian experience with the Pope and to hear his views likewise. The hysterical reaction back in the U.S. was that David was meeting with the Anti-Christ himself in the flesh and Pentecostals were now going to worship the Virgin Mary. Newspapers were complicit in slanted reporting exacerbating the confusion. Part of one of my master's level classes was sorting out the misrepresentations by consulting original sources for the actual exchange of views.

Part of the problem with striving for unity is that each church has its own seminaries or training programs or revered leaders' writings within which students and pastors are expected to learn and socialize. Living within such a bubble one simply can go through life without ever having to consider seriously another's differing view on Scripture. Churches never hire pastors to institute radical change – they hire to preserve their denominational distinctives. Lay people fellowship with other churches most often within their own denomination; those who attend meetings outside their denominational walls are often looked at with suspicion – after all, they might become infected with another church's belief and defect eventually! Insularity unfortunately often breeds contempt for those on the outside.

My better half Susan comes from a Church of Christ background, while I hail from a Pentecostal upbringing. I find it revealing the degree to which bitterness resides even within the confines of one's own denomination. I've had Pentecostals ready to assign me a reservation in the hot places below for not agreeing that speaking in tongues is a necessary component of being a true Christian, or my unwillingness to condemn those who have been water baptized by some other creedal formulation than "in Jesus' name." Susan has witnessed those who have remarried after going through the pain of a divorce being told they are candidates for hellfire, or because they enjoyed listening to instrumental Southern Gospel music.

In our marriage Susan and I have learned to appreciate our different backgrounds while serving Jesus Christ together. We've also learned it's fruitless to argue in an attempt to convince one another on those two or three points in which we sincerely differ. We don't consider those points critically damaging to our walk with Christ or our fellowship; we realize that all Christians have some differences of opinion with each other – otherwise we would all be clones! I've always admired Billy Graham's marriage – his wife is a Presbyterian while Billy is naturally a Baptist. She always supported her husband's ministry 100%, regardless of the fact that she did not see a few points eye-to-eye with her husband. My understanding is that she strongly believed in Calvinism's teachings on predestination, while Billy is a staunch Arminian believer in free-will. They learned to respect each other's differences as well as their love for Christ. That's a pretty good model not only for marriage but for how we view each other in different denominations.

As long as we believe in the basic facts – that Jesus was God's only Son who was crucified, died, buried, and resurrected so that believing on Him we could have forgiveness of sins and eternal life with Him – that's a pretty good basis for unity. Additional church doctrines can be worked out in our respective churches, all the while giving due respect to others who don't see things quite the same way as we do. I don't want everyone to be exactly like me; then I wouldn't be able to garner new insights from others! A world of Steve's would honestly be very boring. Let's learn to appreciate our fellow believers in other camps along with those differences. It's a Godly thing to do.

Disagreeing Agreeably

There is a basic shortcoming that almost everyone in our modern society shares. It's basically an intellectual dishonesty problem. It's more of a process that almost everyone, Christian or non-Christian, participates in almost unknowingly. The results vary from the seemingly benign "pride that I'm right" introspective view, to the devastating "Not only are you a wrong-headed fool but you are inspired by the devil himself" vilifying "Christian" broad-side leveled at people with whom we disagree.

It starts with a rather simple social observation. We enjoy hearing opinions that agree with what we already believe. We want to think of ourselves as reasonably well-raised people with good judgment. Who doesn't? Most people simply don't like disharmony, conflict, intense arguing and debate, and so we don't enjoy inviting opinions that call into question our long-held beliefs. Our beliefs stem from our upbringing, schooling, life experiences, friend's views, parents teachings, church teachings – it's all part of who we are. We almost unconsciously select best friends who share those opinions and beliefs.

What do we do when confronted by an opinion that differs radically from our own? First, there is a physiological response. We emotionally take a step back; our pupils contract; our blood pressure elevates and heart rate increases; our friendly face turns into a rigid unemotional mask or frown; we get that knot in our stomach. Secondly, we start the "process." That involves recollecting every bit of traditional wisdom we have heard on that view in our upbringing that agrees with our own opinion. We defend our opinion with our own personal life experience stories, we quote from our favorite authors, and we will even present statistics if they seem to support our view. We will either use common sense arguments or academic/scientific arguments, depending on which agree with our own perception. We will read articles and books that bolster our view, and listen to the radio talk shows or TV shows that agree with us. We'll even select our news sources to agree with our views in the political world – such as Fox News on the right or the ABC/NBC/CBS news on the left.

What we don't usually do is seriously investigate. We don't usually read books and articles by authors holding the opposite view; listen to TV programs that present the other side, or make it a point to talk about it with people who disagree with us. We are all super-busy these days trying to make a living in a bad economy, be a good parent to our kids, and shuttle from doctor appointments to the hairdresser to the auto repair shop to the gym to the church to the kid's ball game to the restaurant to the mall to the … the list goes on and on. We also suffer from information-overload, with a zillion TV channels to watch, radio stations to listen to, and internet games and blogs. Serious investigation requires a lot of time – precisely what we don't have in our stressed-out lives, or so we think. It's easier and quicker to glance at internet headlines than read a lengthy newspaper article so we cancel our subscription. Scholarly books three inches thick? Forget it. It's also easier to simply shield ourselves from people with opposing viewpoints, much like hitting the "off" button on the remote. It's not as hard on our psyches – no one wants to think they are dead-wrong on a cherished belief.

Moving from the "shut-down" phase we progress to the "criticize" phase – we seemingly have plenty of time for that. Magnify the weak points in someone's proposal while ignoring the strong points. Progressing a little further, we "character assassinate" if we can't handle the viewpoint itself. In the Christian world we take it one further level – we charge the person with the other viewpoint as being inspired by the devil himself. I've received several Emails from people declaring that Obama is the "Anti-Christ in-the-flesh!" Before Obama, liberals resorted to theology-speak in declaring Bush and conservatives as just plain evil.

It appears that our generation is witnessing a loss of the ability to reasonably disagree; to hold a conversation with people of opposing viewpoints courteously and rationally without resorting to that condescending attitude. In the Christian world, there is such a fear of church schisms or members leaving, that courteous debate is considered un-Christian in itself; it is often viewed as divisive or "confusion comes from the devil." That view often prevails notwithstanding that much of Jesus' teachings come to us in the form of vigorous debates with religious peoples of his day, and much of the Apostle Paul's epistles were written in the context of vigorous debate with religious philosophies being promoted in some of the churches to which he was writing. Come to think of it, most of our treasured creedal statements of truth were born out of intensely debated meetings in church councils early in church history. It's the motivation of the individual more than the viewpoint itself that determines whether a person is a strife-making rabble rouser to be shunned or a person seriously seeking the truth about a matter to be heard and seriously considered.

In a culture that is becoming increasingly crude and uncivil, we really need to reacquaint ourselves with basic principles of civility and hospitality with those who disagree with us – especially so in Christianity. Somehow people just don't equate the "speak to the hand" attitude with God's love. The truly empathetic listening ear and exchange of views facilitates a possible change not just in the other person but also in you!

Book of Galatians – Pursue Unity

Sitting at the Buckhead Coffeehouse enjoying a sandwich and an especially good cup of coffee, I was feeling just slightly out-of-place. I had been working hard on my final term paper for "Exegesis of *Galatians*" that day and was up to 5,725 words (all based on ten verses of scripture). My brain needed a rest. I happen to enjoy the ambience of that particular coffeehouse and decided to take a break while eating lunch there. It was a beautiful sunny day and I could almost swear I had heard my old motorcycle calling my name. There's nothing quite like a short bike ride that relaxes my mind and relieves a little bit of stress; perhaps that's the idea behind that bumper sticker I saw that proclaimed "Fire your psychiatrist; buy a motorcycle"!

Sitting in a coffeehouse in black leather biker gear is a bit unusual – you know the stereotype. Bikers are supposed to hang out in smoky bars (at least they used to be smoky) while coffeehouses are the preferred domain of the avant-garde: the artists, literary aficionados, yuppies, college students, and the occasional overweight businessman. Somehow biker leathers are an incongruity in that milieu. Sitting behind me was a well dressed gentleman busily tapping on his laptop – probably a businessman, I thought. I had just been served by a young fellow who looked as though he had just graduated from high school. The two of them apparently knew each other, and their conversation caught my ear. "I'm going to preach out of the book of *Galatians* – I really like the message of grace" explained the young man to the businessman – who actually turned out to be a pastor of a church in Petersburg. I wonder what the odds are on that – taking a break from a study on *Galatians* in a coffeehouse to overhear two preachers discussing *Galatians*?

There was something symbolic in that moment, despite preconceptions and stereotypes – and I'm sure they had one of me! There was an active interest in a 2,000-year-old book and the relevance it had to our modern culture. The Apostle Paul was striving to solve a source of disunity in their church. Paul's opponents (called "agitators" by some scholars) were trying their best to convince these Galatians to pursue a certain course of action – and that entailed submitting to Torah observance (especially the Law of Moses in the Old Testament) such as the rite of circumcision, kosher food purity laws, and observance of special days in the Jewish calendar. These were boundary markers that helped identify the people of God in a Jewish setting; they were considered essential to national Jewish identity. The problem was that the Galatians were not Jewish, they were Gentiles (non-Jewish). The agitators were trying to persuade these Gentiles that they really couldn't be bono fide members of God's family unless they lived like Jews.

Paul had been spreading the gospel message among the Gentiles in the Mediterranean world without any obligation required of his converts to "be Jewish." To enforce such a requirement would have immediately introduced a source of disunity in the early Christian church; a prime example involved the Apostle Peter himself in his unfortunate withdrawing of social contact with Gentiles – he wouldn't even eat with them (Galatians 2:12). For the church to grow unhindered unity must prevail, and thus the motivator for Paul's writing of this letter to the Galatian Christians.

That social situation is really not all that different from our social situation 2,000 years later here in America. There is a common thread of thought that I have noticed among both churched and unchurched people I have talked with – people are a little sick of the old denominational strife over doctrine and attempts to proselytize each other's members. It sets a bad example to those who question the Christian faith, to start with; their feeling is "if all these Christians do is argue with each other, I don't want anything to do with it." Instead of working together in bringing the glorious message of God's grace to a discouraged and cynical world, we sometimes resemble competitive poker players jealously eyeballing each other's pile of chips – who's got the biggest congregation now? It's a shame we make more of a fuss over the 20% we don't see eye-to-eye on rather than the 80% that we agree on. When different denominations start finding causes they can mutually support and work together on, that's when skeptics might sit up and take notice. Unity – it's still worth pursuing 2,000 years later.

Judgment Calls – "Blessing of the Animals"

There are certain times in every honest person's life that he or she has to eat "humble pie." It's especially important to us as Christians since we are supposed to quickly admit our mistakes and faults with a sense of humility about ourselves as Christ taught. One of those moments came for me when I read about the "Blessing of the Animals" held recently at St. John's Episcopal Church. In years past I would have shook my head sadly about such an event. My attitude was quite condescending: "Don't they realize that the gospel is all about people, not animals?" and "Jesus and His disciples never went around blessing animals" would have been a couple of statements I would have made.

After reading the account of the "Blessing of the Animals" in Friday's edition, I recalled a time in my childhood in which I prayed for my pet dog. I had almost forgotten about that. My pet dog had contracted a horrible case of that "croup" type of cough that dogs get and was getting really weak. Dad was too frugal to take our pet to the veterinarian, so I figured my dog's fate was sealed. In desperation I prayed for that dog and by the next day his cough was gone; his strength fully returned shortly thereafter. The same thing happened with a dog my dad owned about fifteen years later. The poor mutt was horribly sick and weak, so my sister and I prayed for it; two days later it was completely well.

A couple of years ago I wrote an article about a baby robin that had fallen out of its nest and landing on a hard bench below, with its little head dangling between the wooden slats. There was no breathing or sign of life, but I put it back in the nest anyway and said a prayer for it. When I returned from work later that day it was happily nestled with its sibling, begging for worms. I'm sure that an agnostic or atheist would argue for simple statistical probability in all these cases. Each animal just happened to get well and my prayers preceding the event were just coincidental; however, I've heard too many similar stories told by others to acquiesce to that line of reasoning. In all these cases someone might say "Stephen, you prayed for an Animal Blessing didn't you?" I would have responded "Yes, but those were dire cases, not general blessings." A mite bit of equivocation sometimes soothes a pricked conscience.

In the Old Testament God blessed a believer named Jacob by increasing the fertility of his flock of goats (Genesis 31). Blessings for Israel's obedience included blessings on their livestock – "the calves of your herds and the lambs of your flocks" (Deuteronomy 28:4). I would have responded "Yes, but that was their livelihood." God apparently was concerned enough about animals to include a verse about them in Proverbs 12:10 — "A righteous man cares for the needs of his animals…" If I am a pet owner and don't take good care of my pet, then my very righteousness is called into question. That's getting personal!

There is a very important hermeneutical (common sense rule of Biblical interpretation) observation that goes something like this: "What is not specifically addressed in Scripture can neither be made doctrinally necessary nor banned outright; it may require a judgment call in relation to broader Biblical principles or common sense." For those who ignore this rule, I have a question: just where does the Bible describe what is to be done in a marriage ceremony or funeral ceremony and by whom? There are no such rules, just a recording of what was commonly done in the culture at that time; these things vary tremendously across different cultures today. Try telling your preacher or pastor that he should immediately stop doing marriage or funeral ceremonies because there is no record of Jesus and the Apostles performing them! Most churches today consider those functions to be very necessary even though Scripture does not specifically address how or by whom.

Good Christians may have very different ideas about whether pets have souls like people or whether they can go to heaven; I tend to think they don't, but famous ministers like Billy Graham presently and Martin Luther in the 16th century would disagree with me – they fully expect to see their pet dog when they get there. It's best to leave things like this and Animal Blessings to a believer's conscience and local church practice. Let's not sweat the small stuff but rather strive to understand other Christians of a different stripe a little better.

SOCIAL DRINKING – OK?

Teetotalers versus Social Drinkers

Ron Hart writes some pretty interesting and humorous articles. We tend to see alike on economic conservatism, but we vary widely on social issues — Ron's a Libertarian, and I'm a traditional social conservative. Ron's last article was about social drinking, and he asked a question of me when he sent it my way for editing — was his view of drinking alcohol in moderation consistent with Biblical Christian belief? It's a good question, and various Protestant denominations have taken different stands on that issue historically.

I was raised in a teetotaling church that preached you were sinning if you drank a drop of alcohol. They would quote scriptures that warned against the evils of drunkenness. We would "tsk-tsk" and shake our heads at those older mainline denominations' members who socially drank, or the Catholics with their beer tents up north in Michigan where we lived. "If they only knew their Bibles better," we thought. Actually, we needed to know our own Bibles better.

There are four Greek words translated as "wine" in the New Testament: oinos, gleu-kos, paroinos, oinophlugia; each of these by Greek definition refer to fermented grape juice. In those days there was no refrigeration or pasteurization, and grape juice quickly fermented in the hot environs of Middle Eastern villages. Jesus' first miracle was changing water into wine at a wedding. The old argument about "wine" really meaning "grape juice" in some cases is simply bad scholarship — not only by Greek definitions, but also by literary context.

When the host of the wedding banquet tasted the water turned into wine *(John 2:10)* he remarked "Everyone brings out the choice wine first and then the cheaper wine after the guests have had too much to drink; but you have saved the best till now." Grape juice doesn't dim a person's judgment, but too much wine will indeed. To be logically consistent, our fundamentalist church would have to believe that Jesus' first miracle induced sinning. I've examined all thirty-seven usages of "wine" in the New Testament, and none of them prohibit drinking alcoholic wine, they only warn of drunkenness. Alcoholic wine was customarily used in first-century Jewish culture, especially at festive occasions such as weddings.

On the other hand, our modern culture here in the U.S. is nothing like first century Jewish culture. They didn't have a high rate of alcoholism; we do. Semitic peoples don't have the genetic risk factor associated with alcoholism that some other ethnic groups do have today. This is a medical fact; ask your doctor. They didn't have refrigeration and pasteurization; we do. They didn't normally drink to get a buzz or forget their troubles or lower their date's inhibitions — while many Americans do.

They didn't have high-speed automobiles; we do. About the worst that could happen back then is that your donkey might have a head-on collision with the other guy's donkey. Driver education courses will tell you that just one beer will start affecting your judgment and reaction time. Our hypocritical culture warns us of the dangers of drinking and driving while portraying having a good social time at the neighborhood bar with friends as normal. How do we get there? Driving our vehicles. Americans are very individualistic and independent; car-pooling has never really caught on. We value highly driving our own personal vehicles to our destinations.

If the fundamentalist churches are guilty of inferior Biblical scholarship on this issue and ignoring first-century Jewish culture, then more traditional mainline denominations are likewise sometimes guilty of ignoring the dangers of social drinking in a very different modern American culture. When Hollywood stars, famous athletes, political incumbents, and other role models are caught driving drunk, and so many American families are devastated by alcoholism, isn't that a sin that needs to be highlighted occasionally in church services? That's if they still preach on sin. Sounds old-fashioned and fundamental, doesn't it?

Alcoholism and Genetics

I well remember the first time I tried to drink. It was a cheap bottle of Gallo wine and I was just shy of my twentieth birthday. Back then it was legal at the age of 18 – society figured if you were old enough to get married and be sent off in a war to die for your country then you were old enough to drink. All my life I had been warned at church not to drink a drop of alcohol and a common part of the dedicatory prayer offered for newborn infants involved praying "may their lips never know the taste of a cigarette or alcohol." That may be considered rather odd for churches now-a-days, but we were a small sect of Pentecostals and we viewed alcohol as though there was a demon in every bottle and that first sip was guaranteeing a life of sin in alcoholism with a one way ticket to the infernal regions below. Well, maybe those baby dedication prayers worked because I thought it tasted like a rat had crawled up into that bottle and died. The same happened later with beer – it tasted purely awful.

Obviously I've never had a problem with alcohol but I've known several good, smart, do-anything-to-help-you-out friends who have struggled greatly in trying to kick the bottle. Their stories are filled with the emotional pain, embarrassment, and a sense of pervasive failure that comes out of those struggles. I've interviewed the presidents of both Teen Challenge and the Place of Hope here in Columbia and written articles about the wonderful work these organizations do in helping residents kick the alcohol habit.

We presently know a whole lot more about what's involved in alcoholism than we did when I was a child, both medically and theologically. Back in my childhood days, all you had to do to get a Pentecostal really riled up was suggest that Jesus' first miracle involved turning the water into alcoholic wine, and they would inevitably argue up a blue streak that it was really nothing more than grape juice. Of course they had to ignore a few other scriptures that actually encouraged the use of alcohol such as Deuteronomy 14:26, Proverbs 9:5, and Isaiah 25:6, but a lot of church going folks do that quite regularly – quote the verses they like and ignore the ones they don't like. Most Christians today acknowledge that the sin is in drinking to excess and having a glass of wine with a meal can't be condemned. Most also realize that the modern risk of driving high speed automobiles under the influence is far greater than driving your donkeys under the influence.

If anyone had suggested back then that certain groups of people are predisposed to alcoholism more so than other people because of their genetic make-up, we would have thought they were nuts or were trying to justify the sin of alcoholism. That is now considered to be a fact. The National Institute on Alcohol Abuse and Alcoholism states that "the familial transmission of alcoholism risk is at least in part genetic" which has been verified by identical and fraternal twin studies. The American Academy of Child & Adolescent Psychiatry has found that children of alcoholics are four more times likely than other children to become alcoholics, and a likely culprit that is being investigated is the A1 allele of the DRD2 gene. It has also been shown that certain groups of people – such as Asians – have "two genes that protect against heavy drinking" while groups such as Euro-Americans, Eskimos, and Native Americans do not have these protective genes, according to the Indiana Alcohol Research Center. The gene for enzyme aldehyde dehydrogenase in Asian populations delays the liver from converting even small amounts of alcohol into acetate, which results in rapid heartbeat, headache, nausea, flushing of the face, and extreme drowsiness which is a really good deterrent to alcoholism.

Even if you are predisposed to being at greater risk to alcoholism, that doesn't excuse you from the necessity of fighting it – for your health's sake, your children's sake, and society's sake with whom you share the highway. Yes, it's still a sin. What I find logically inconsistent is for people to argue that being gay is purely genetic (which has never been proved) and that therefore "God makes you gay" and there is nothing wrong with it. There is definitely a genetic component to many people's alcoholism but no one argues that "God made them that way and it's ok." That, I suspect, is a cultural double standard due purely to liberal social pressure in our society.

ILLEGAL IMMIGRATION

Illegal Immigration Issue

I was on my way home the other day from a VFW hall reflecting on my first-time experience of a Mexican style graduation party for a young lady. Photos of her at various stages of life, including graduation, adorned a display board; spicy chicken and tortillas were being served to hungry friends and relatives; loud strains of festive music were emanating from an adjoining room with that multi-colored flashing light ambience that reminded me of the old discos back in the 70's. The songs and the conversation were mostly in Spanish, making me wish I had continued in those Spanish courses in college. As one of only five gringos in the whole place, I was never made to feel unwelcome and the friend I had gone with was hugged and warmly greeted by those who knew her personally. It was a family friendly event as is typical of Mexican culture; seeing a grandpa holding his grandson on the dance floor gently swaying to the music was touching.

Reflecting on those pleasant thoughts while waiting to make a left turn off Bear Creek Pike to drop my friend off, I noticed something rather unpleasant – headlights approaching rapidly from the rear and not slowing down. "Is he going to stop?" I wondered — another glance at the mirror confirmed my horrible premonition. "Hold on" I yelled bracing for impact – a very loud "crash" with a body-jolting and instant-headache catapulting thrust forward. The first thing I noticed after coming to my senses was the loud hissing of steam from their radiator. We had been rear-ended by a small SUV that never even made an attempt to stop.

My friend had a concussion; I stumbled out of my truck to see if I could help the other driver who was surely in worse shape; there was no other driver. The other vehicle was empty except for beer bottles on the floorboard – they had bailed and run off into the night. Soon the police, fire trucks, and ambulances were there directing traffic and transporting my friend to Maury Regional Medical Center. The one statement that still rings in my ears came from a police officer who said "We see these accidents quite often where the driver flees and often it's an illegal immigrant." A drunk or an illegal or both, I thought.

That memorable day brought home to me in a personal way the opposite views on legal versus illegal immigration. I've heard all the startling statistics concerning the stress on our social services, the drug trade, gang activities, and drunken driving with no license or insurance or ability to read English road signs. I've also met many God-fearing, clean living, hard working and family oriented Mexicans who, to my surprise, turned out to be illegals. I've heard all the arguments about how they are willing to do much of the hard manual labor that most Americans disdain. Their biggest vice often seems to be sending disposable income back to destitute relatives in Mexico.

Immigration reform has turned into a political football, while most Americans agree something has to be done – but just what engenders endless debate. To grant instant amnesty to hard working Mexican families most of whom hold to conservative values similar to mine has a certain appeal to me, but it seems patently unfair to all the other nationalities who are forced to wait years in a very expensive legal immigration process.

I don't have an obvious solution and neither does Obama, Clinton, or McCain. On a personal level, I try to keep an open mind and a non-judgmental spirit towards the Mexicans I meet personally. The ones who flout our laws and are found to be illegal should be immediately jailed and deported – and I don't think that's racist.

Securing our borders is not a bad idea — nations incapable of doing so usually don't remain nations very long. Working towards a path to citizenship for otherwise law abiding, hard working, family oriented Mexicans while securing borders at the same time seems like a good idea also; believing this does not make me a doormat liberal. Working for a solution nationally while extending a hand of friendship to Mexicans you know personally seems to me an appropriate Christian response.

Border Control

It was back in the late 70's when I first became personally acquainted with Lebanese Christians. A brutal civil war was raging in Lebanon, and a Christian family had immigrated to the U.S. to escape the fighting. They began attending our church in Michigan; we reached out to them in Christian love with full acceptance. The liaison for the family and Christian minister, Mr. Rababy (they were his relatives) spoke fluent English while the family spoke mainly Arabic. I remember feeling deep sympathy for a family that was forced to leave their country, culture, and language far behind to live in near social isolation in my country. Mr. Rababy was a guest in our home once, and I still vividly remember his returned hospitality – coffee. He had his own little private stock of coffee beans and his own little grinder. He brought it with him and hand-ground coffee beans and percolated some of the most flavorful, and strongest, coffee I had ever tasted. I also vividly remember his love for Jesus Christ. Sometimes we forget about the Christian communities that have lived in the Middle East for over a thousand years.

I've never had a problem with foreigners immigrating to the United States, as long as they do so legally and respect our laws and customs. I do have a major concern, however, for unrestricted illegal immigration coming through our southern border – and not because I have any bias against Mexicans. It was about two years ago I wrote a column detailing my concern of how easy it would be for exporters of radical Islam to slip through our porous southern border, and I took a little heat for that column. Where was the evidence, and how would that be possible?

A few weeks ago a Lebanese Christian lady testified before Congress about that very subject. Brigitte Gabriel was raised in southern Lebanon and knows first-hand the horrors of Islamic Jihad. She and her family were forced to live in a bomb shelter for seven years during Lebanon's civil war. Her house was destroyed and all her childhood friends were killed by Islamic militias. Later in life she became a TV news anchorwoman for *World News*, which is broadcast in Arabic throughout Egypt, Israel, Jordan, Syria, Lebanon, and Cyprus (she speaks fluent Arabic, French, English, and Hebrew). She has contributed news stories to all the major American news networks along with *20/20, Good Morning America, The History Channel, TLC, Discovery Channel, Oprah Winfrey Show*, etc. Brigitte lectures internationally about terrorism, and is author of the book "Because They Hate: A Survivor of Islamic Terror Warns America." She basically warned Congress about the easy penetration of our southern border by Islamic radicals who achieve that feat by teaming-up with the MS-13 street gang.

It's not a far-right pipe dream. Back on January 5th of 2005, the *Boston Herald* reported that the MS-13 East Boston street gang "has been linked to the Al-Qaeda terrorist network prompting Boston police to 'turn up the heat' on its members." It was March of that same year that Congressman Solomon Ortiz (D-Texas) testified that Al-Qaeda "offers about $250,000 to smuggle high value Al-Qaeda operatives across the border." Mr. Ortiz is a member of the House Armed Services Committee which oversees national security. It was Feb. 24th of this current year that a MS-13 gang member was arrested attempting to smuggle three illegal aliens into the U.S. The FBI has reported that there are about 30,000 MS-13 gang members in the U.S., and in the southwestern U.S. they thrive on smuggling drugs and people for profit. It was in March of this year that the chief officer of the American Consulate in Matamoros, John Naland, expressed his concern about Al-Qaeda getting help from Central American Mara Salvatrucha gang members (MS-13).

It's not rocket science. Saudi Arabia spends billions of dollars (courtesy of you and me every time we "fill-er-up") spreading radical Wahhabi Islamic literature and schools all over the world which preach hatred and Jihad against the Evil West. With large sums of money being offered to transport an operative and gang members willing to do just about anything for money, opportunity eventually comes knocking. When they get here, they will have a receptive audience. A recent poll by the New York Post found that "one of four young Muslims in the U.S. believe suicide bombings against innocent civilians are OK." There are around 2.4 million Muslims currently residing in the United States.

It's time to take border control seriously instead of making it into a political football. Your very own future security may depend on it.

DIVINE HEALING: WHEN BAD THEOLOGY BECOMES REAL TRAGEDY

It's terrible and tragic and it happens about every year. The really unfortunate aspect is that it is entirely preventable. A simple phone call would prevent a needless untimely death of a precious child, but the phone call never happens in time because the parents are playing God. It boils down to bad theology.

The latest incident was the death of 11-year-old Madeline Neuman in Wisconsin. She became deathly ill starting with weakness, then a fever, and then her legs turned blue. The weakness was so bad she would fall off the commode when she visited the bathroom. Eventually she couldn't even sit up in bed, then she couldn't talk or drink water. The last stage was a coma. She died from diabetic ketoacidosis, and it was very treatable with insulin. Her parents never called 911 because they thought it was a spiritual attack; they do not believe in traditional medical care but rather believe that all healing comes through personal prayer. Her father, Dale Neumann, stated "If I go to the doctor, I am putting the doctor before God." Her mother, Leilani Neumann, wanted to make sure the public knew that "they are not crazy, religious people" and that their family does not claim any official membership in any organized religion or faith.

Well I doubt that either parent would meet the qualifications for the certifiable crazy status, but I suspect they are very religious indeed along with being sincerely deluded in regard to the "doctors are bad" rule. Dale once studied to be a Pentecostal minister, and one family member described the Neumanns as Pentecostal; they were getting ready to start a ministry at their coffee shop. Both parents have been convicted of second-degree reckless homicide and face up to twenty-five years in prison.

A word of caution is in order before we tar and feather entire Pentecostal denominations. I was raised in a Pentecostal church, and if anyone was seriously ill, we believed in getting them to the doctor pronto. If it was an accident or emergency, we would be the first calling 911 for the ambulance. Yes, we believed in prayer and that God can still do miracles, but we prayed while the patient was on the way to the hospital, while they were there, and that God would direct the physician's hands. We viewed doctors as being on our side. Both the church and the hospital were working for the same end – a healthy patient.

There are a few oddball Pentecostal and Word of Faith churches that teach the "every Christian should be divinely healed through faith" doctrine along with the "you are showing a lack of faith if you go to a doctor" brand of belief. I've been in a few of those churches in years past and the funny thing is even the leaders and pastors occasionally have to go for medical help, especially when they get older, but it's all "hush-hush" – the church members aren't supposed to know! But of course if anyone breaks their leg or is giving birth to a child, they immediately rush to the hospital – showing the illogicality of their position.

Jesus had no harsh words for physicians of his day 2,000 years ago, as primitive as the medical profession was back then. He used the well-known proverb "It is not the healthy who need a doctor but the sick" (Matthew 9:12) as representative of his own restorative ministry. The books of Luke and Acts were written by a physician (Colossians 4:14). The very same Apostle Paul who had healed multitudes on various occasions could not heal his son in the faith Timothy, but rather had to give him some medical advice for his stomach problems (1 Timothy 5:23). Paul himself later had a medical problem with his own eyes (Galatians 4:13-15; 6:11).

Coming from a Pentecostal background I have to walk a fine line between knowing for a fact that healing miracles do occasionally happen which are unexplainable by modern science while warning against the dangers of "don't go to a doctor, just pray and believe" theology. The former are rarely printed by newspapers due to the difficulty of verification and because editors do not want to look unprofessional or unscientific. The latter can have disastrous consequences as with poor little Madeline Neumann. There are certain symptoms that accompany possible heart attacks or strokes that can be helped, absent a miracle, only if the person is rushed to the hospital immediately.

I personally know what it's like to be divinely, miraculously healed as a young man – but it's doubtful *The Daily Herald* would print it. I also know that if it were not for doctors I would be dead or severely crippled by now. I've had three medically necessary operations in my later years – two congenital defects and back surgery. As a young man I was a new Christian; in my later years I've grown in the faith through years of living for Christ and Bible study, so don't tell me it's a lack of faith.

Let's resist the temptation to play God and realize that God is sovereign. Sometimes He does a genuine miracle, but often He does not. Sometimes he uses men and women that He has called into the medical profession to use their talents to help the ill and injured. How friendly is your church to physicians and nurses as members? Would they feel welcome? Would Luke the physician, writer of the books of Luke and Acts, have been welcome in your church? It's something to think about.

MARRIAGE AND CHRISTIANITY

Marriage – a Dying Institution?

Marriage is a soon-to-be dead institution – it's history. That's the conclusion one might draw reading *USA Today's* article on November 18 entitled "Nearly 40% say marriage is becoming obsolete." That poll taken by the Pew Research Center also cited a cohabitation rate (what folks tend to call "shacking up," or as with my generation, "fornication") that stands at 44% of adults saying they have cohabitated. Many of the younger generation claim that marriage is just a piece of paper, and with so many TV sitcoms and movies belittling traditional marriage, but promoting gay marriage, of course, perhaps we should be surprised that headlines like this one haven't been trumpeted and endlessly debated much earlier.

Sometimes it all in the way the statistics are presented. The headline didn't phrase it like this: "60% say marriage is very important and 56% have never cohabitated, believing it to be wrong." That wouldn't sell as many newspapers. There has been, however, a dramatic shift in our American society since the ideal Cleaver family was idolized in my grandparent's day. Back then there were no birth control pills and large families were the norm. Women could not prevent pregnancy and therefore did not enter the workforce in large numbers in pursuit of personal careers.

Men were expected to marry and be the breadwinners; women were expected to marry young and tend to the large brood of children without all the labor-saving modern conveniences in the kitchen and laundry room. Christian moral standards prevailed; sex outside of marriage was stigmatized, while horrible STD's could only be avoided by remaining sexually pure until marriage. Unintended pregnancies outside of marriage often ended in "shotgun marriages." The vast majority of people married in their early twenties and if you waited much longer than that, you would have found a very small pool of prospective marriage partners. Being single was almost viewed as a curse.

The differences today are startling. Birth control separated reproduction from sex and society eventually came to see the pursuit of sex as being for pleasure rather than for having kids. Large families are now frowned upon, with most couples wanting two children at the most. Women are more numerous in our universities than men and view their careers as being very important so as not to be dependent solely on a man. Christian morals have been relegated to a prior Victorian era for the most part while many young people now view having sex as a prerequisite to even thinking about possible marriage – sort of a "trying out" period. Rather than being forced through societal pressure to marry, many are having a hard time finding partners willing to marry. Most STD's can be treated or prevented now.

There is actually now a fear of being married – many young people have witnessed first-hand the dissolution of their parent's marriage with all the turmoil and heartbreak it entails. Divorces per 1,000 marriages were about 140 in 1969; 380 in 1990; and a whopping 451 in 1996. Financial devastation often accompanies the divorce – for both partners, but usually worse for women. Divorce now stands as the number one factor correlated to suicide rates in large U.S. cities according to The National Institute for

Healthcare Research. Other studies show that divorcees are twice as likely to suffer from a mental illness; 75% of their children end up in divorce; their children's drop-out rate from school is twice the average; and the best predictor of teen suicide is living with a divorced parent. Is there any wonder why many are fearful of tying the knot?

Despite the fear, the good news is that same Pew survey revealed that only 13% of respondents indicated they never had a desire to marry – and for a bit of perspective that percentage is less than the number of Americans who believe the sun revolves around the earth (18%!!!). A politician who had 87% of the vote would loudly proclaim they had a "mandate from the people," so I doubt that the institution of marriage is going to completely die out anytime soon. Even 60% of the co-habiting couples expressed a desire to eventually take the plunge. Desire is demonstrably different from behavior – they are simply scared.

This is an excellent opportunity for churches and other social organizations to step into the gap and teach, counsel, and role model the crucial skills that are necessary for being successful marriage partners and good parents. For too long we have simply ignored the subject and gossiped when church members were going through martial disharmony. Our loving Creator has instilled into human hearts the craving for companionship – to love and be loved. Marriage – it's still worth honoring and fighting for.

Why are Christian Marriages Failing?

Marriage — most everyone you meet here in the South will agree with (or at least pay lip service to) the concept that marriage is a foundational cornerstone to good civilization. Evangelical Christians especially emphasize the importance of marriage because the sanctity and God-directed purpose of marriage is repeatedly portrayed in Scripture. The link between broken marriages and poverty, depression, suicide and violence toward estranged spouses has been clearly shown by sociologists. Often the ones who are completely innocent suffer the most — the children.

The problem is that despite the obvious, marriage is in big trouble here in the United States. Sociologist Brad Wilcox of the University of Virginia has noted that "In the last 40 years, marriage rates have plummeted, illegitimacy and divorce have surged and cohabitation has become fashionable."[23] It is common knowledge that America now has a higher divorce rate at nearly 50 percent than any of the other modern industrialized countries of the world. The world's only remaining superpower is seemingly powerless to preserve the basic institution of marriage. When half of all the people you meet have already or will be divorced, it's little wonder that young people are so reluctant to take the plunge — especially when many of them have seen the heart-rending consequences of marital dissolution in their own parents' lives. They are simply scared.

The really startling statistic is that the divorce rate is basically the same in the Christian community as it is in the secular community. That seems to be a painfully obvious contradiction since the New Testament emphasis on loving one's spouse "as Christ loved the church" in a selfless, even sacrificial, way is the model taught but apparently not often practiced. Jesus' instructions on the importance of forgiveness, love, responsibility, and divorce only in non-reconcilable instances of marital infidelity would produce a very low divorce rate in the Christian community — one would think.

This bitter irony has been noted by those on the political left who portray conservative Christians as being hypocritical — moralizing on the sinfulness of gay marriages while divorcing at the same rate as non-Christians. The old "When all else fails read the instructions" saying applies here; it is indeed a shame that so many of us are failing in the application of good biblical principles, but that doesn't imply that we should throw-away the instruction manual.

I have long suspected that some of the same factors leading to our high divorce rate are nonreligious — present in both believers' and nonbelievers' marriages. Sociologists and psychologists now seem to be proving that assumption correct.

Glenn T. Stanton, author of "Why Marriage Matters: Reasons to Believe in Marriage in Postmodern Society," has noted that the most prevalent factors which contribute to marital success are "higher income, increased education level, higher age at marriage."[24] That seems to be common sense; if you are constantly arguing over money or the lack thereof along with a good dose of ignorance and immaturity, then the possibility of divorce increases dramatically.

Family therapists have observed another pattern in marital counseling. Putting the different observations into the form of a common story, it goes something like this from the wife's perspective: "My marriage seemed to be just fine years ago, but has changed very slowly for the worst. My husband comes home exhausted every night because he is working longer hours. It seems as though he is married to his employment. When he gets a few days off work, he usually spends it playing golf or watching television rather than interacting with me. Romantic dinners and intimate conversations are nothing but dim memories. The emotional closeness between us seems to have evaporated. He still has a priority in having his sexual desires satisfied, but it doesn't seem to bother him that the emotional closeness is not there. Sex has become sort of a business relationship. The compassion, understanding, communication, the sweet whispers in my ear – it has all been replaced by 'doing my sexual duty.' I honestly feel like a prostitute. The idea of 'being used' by my spouse has me so depressed that I'm seriously considering divorce."

Marriages are not simply business propositions and it's a shame when romance slowly dies through neglect. It's not that Christian commitment is unimportant — I believe it's hugely important. It's simply tragic when another "used to be" good marriage dies from not "tending the vine" of emotional warmth and romance. Don't be another statistic — tend that vine.

DOES SPANKING PROMOTE VIOLENCE?

Quick – let's do a word association test. What group of people do you think of when I say the word "non-violent"? I could say "non-aggressive" or "peaceful" or other synonyms, but what segment of our society comes to mind with those descriptors? For me personally I usually think of the Amish or Mennonites. They may be on the fringes of our American society, but I can't think of a more peaceful group of people. You will never see headlines like "Amish man robs pharmacy at gunpoint escaping in a very fast buggy" or "Mennonite goes postal at the mall, killing seventeen people." Visit your local prison and see how many Amish or Mennonites you can find in residence there. They are so peaceful they won't retaliate when provoked and refuse to fight even in self defense. They are true pacifists, meaning they refuse military service.

According to modern liberal thinking, we should all learn to emulate their non-violent ways. Oh, by the way, they are strong believers in corporal punishment for their children. Surprised? Adults consider it a priority to "break the will of the child" at an early age – when the child becomes self-aware. Discipline becomes a norm at about the age of two, and the use of spanking is encouraged if needed – verified in a study by Hostetler and Huntington in 1992. To the "spanking teaches violence and leads to aggressive violent adults" advocates this simply doesn't make sense.

It's not just in our society that such a "contradiction" can be found. Once in a while we hear news reports of some American visiting Singapore being "caned" for violating a local law in that country. "Oh the horror of such brutality" is what we usually think without considering what their society is like. They are "extreme spankers" – very abusive by our Western standards. Parents regularly "cane" their children for discipline, teachers in their schools do the same, and jailers cane their unruly inmates. By our liberal logic, Singapore should be one of the most violent societies on earth. Singapore is actually one of the most non-violent of modern industrial societies with violence rates below Sweden's in many areas. Juvenile delinquency and vandalism is almost non-existent; children perform well on academic achievement tests; women walk the streets alone without fearing being assaulted or raped. It just doesn't make sense to the "ban spanking" crowd. By the way, speaking of Sweden – violence between minors and child abuse has increased 600% in 15 years since banning all spanking in the home in 1979.

I don't mind the ban-spanking advocates voicing their opinions or arguing their case in the media, as long as it's done in a respectful manner. What I do mind is misusing a scientific study to support banning corporal punishment – to knowingly skew a study's findings to support one's opinion, or the intentional ignoring of many other scientific studies which show opposite findings. That is journalism at its worst – closely related to propaganda.

Anna Quindlen related the findings of a study in her article "A teachable moment: Honesty in parenting" which was quite less than honest, methodologically speaking (*The Daily Herald*, April 23). That study by Laurie Miller Brotman showed that troubled kids became less aggressive and were developing more normally after being involved in a child-training program that utilized "consistent discipline without corporal punishment, positive reinforcement for good behavior." The kids cortisol levels even changed to more normal thus showing social intervention can change biology. The problem is using this study to imply that science has shown corporal punishment to be counterproductive.

One of the first things I learned in pursuing a Bachelor of Science degree many years ago is the importance of carefully controlling independent and dependent variables. To study corporal punishment you would need to keep all other variables the same between the experimental and control group and vary only the corporal punishment in the experimental group. Obviously such was not done; Laurie Brotman's study taught parents "new behavioral skills that promote positive behavior" such as "to praise children's social skills, and ignore and punish misbehavior" ("Questions and Answers with Laurie Brotman, Ph.D." from the Langone Medical Center). Laurie claimed no such "scientific evidence disproving the value of spanking" for her study.

Iowa State researchers have concluded that "the level of parental support and involvement with children, not corporal punishment, predicted negative outcomes" (August 1994 of *Journal of Marriage and the Family*). They also noted that anti-spanking studies "suffer from serious methodological limitations" including "sampling, measurement, and failure to utilize control groups." Dr. Robert Larzelere of Oklahoma State University and Brett Kuhn of the University of Nebraska Medical Center reviewed several different anti-spanking studies and came to the same conclusion – actually finding spanking to be an effective disciplinary technique for 2 to 6 year olds when other milder disciplinary measures had failed (*Clinical Child and Family Psychology Review*, 2005).

If you are going to use a scientific study to support your opinion as a journalist, know the methodology well enough to draw valid conclusions and don't ignore contrary evidence. Even liberals can agree with that, I hope!

PROSTITUTION — THE "VICTIMLESS CRIME"?

I've never been a big soccer fan. It may be "football" to the rest of the world, but it just doesn't compare to "football" here in terms of entertainment value for me personally. While soccer fans went crazy as Italy won it all at the World Cup hosted by Germany, another spectator sport was stealing the show — legalized prostitution. Germany legalized prostitution in 2002, and had constructed sex huts — sort of like fancy porta-potties around the stadiums. Apparently the 400,000 legal prostitutes weren't enough, so the "State pimp" had issued extra prostitution licenses to incoming foreign prostitutes to meet demand at the games, and accordingly built little sex huts to accommodate them.

Liberals and Libertarians in this country have always viewed anything relating to individual sexuality as being beyond the proper bounds of our government's interference. They claim that prostitution is going to exist anyway, legal or illegal. Many of them view the laws criminalizing prostitution as an old-fashioned leftover from a prior Christianized world view, a view out-of-step with modern societies. They would tout the benefits of legalization, such as taxation and the regulation of health services for the women involved (or men!). They would view the Scandinavian countries as progressive, and would undoubtedly applaud Germany's decision.

President Bush isn't applauding, and neither is U.S. Secretary of State Condoleezza Rice; both have promised to bring international public pressure on Germany. A lot of U.S. House of Representatives legislators are not applauding. House resolution 860, sponsored by Rep. Chris Smith from New Jersey, implores Germany to take action towards stopping sex trafficking at the World Cup. Condoleezza Rice stated that "The United States is leading a new abolitionist movement to end the sordid trade in human beings." "Wait a minute," liberals are saying.

What's this talk about sex trafficking and sordid trade? Women sold or forced into prostitution is a different issue; Nicholas Kristof of *The New York Times* wrote that anti-trafficking measures targeting legal prostitution are a ridiculously divisive sideshow not germane to the central challenge of sex trafficking. Prostitution, they say, is a victimless crime. The customers are willing and the prostitutes are simply engaging in a business to meet the demand.

Prostitution is hardly victimless — the victims are the prostitutes themselves. The U.S. State Department did field research in nine countries and found that "60 to 75 percent of women in prostitution were raped, 70 to 95 percent were physically assaulted, and 68 percent met the criteria for post-traumatic stress disorder in the same range as treatment-seeking combat veterans and victims of state-organized torture." The world's oldest profession is a misnomer; it should be the world's oldest oppression. A rather poignant concluding statement was that "Prostitution leaves women and children physically, mentally and spiritually devastated." The study also noted that 89 percent of respondents desired to leave the business.

What much of the public doesn't know is that legal prostitution and sexual slavery are inextricably linked; the former facilitating the latter. What happens is that girls from countries like Russia or the Ukraine answer newspaper ads that promise a job or training courses in a major European city. They often use fake passports to get there, and upon arrival are stunned to hear that the jobs are already filled, or the school has closed, and they owe $10,000 to their handlers which of course they cannot pay. They are beaten, raped and forced into prostitution to repay their debt. Often they are transferred to another pimp in a legal red-light district such as the one in Brussels. If they escape and contact police, they are jailed because of lack of documentation. It is estimated that the sexual slavery business takes in around $7 billion annually, and also estimated that many of those 40,000 prostitutes shipped into Germany for the World Cup were poor Eastern Europeans who had fallen prey to organized crime.

President Bush, Condoleezza Rice and the supporters of U.S. House bill 860 are right on this issue. It's time to draw the veil back from prostitution to see it for what it really is — harmful, degrading, and definitely linked to organized crime. Modern states should not be in the pimping business, and greed for tax monies is no excuse for facilitating the world's oldest oppression.

WORLD OVERPOPULATION – MENACE OR MYTH?

Every once in a while it takes a reader's comment to Ann Landers to jolt my awareness of a major social societal issue that had been slipping under the radar of my perception. Recently a reader opined in an Ann Lander's column that parents with many children should feel ashamed of themselves for contributing to the overpopulation of our planet. Such short-sightedness supposedly is a reason for natural resource depletion, increased pollution, overcrowding and poverty, along with an unsustainable human population growth worldwide. To top it off such large families are condoned by religious reasoning along with a disapproval of birth control practices such as contraception.

There is a grain of truth in that reader's opinion. Some churches teach that contraception is wrong, that it is interfering with a natural process that God is in charge of. They point to scriptures such as Genesis 1:28: "Be fruitful and increase in number; fill the earth and subdue it" or Psalms 127:4-5: "Like arrows in the hands of a warrior are sons born in one's youth. Blessed is the man whose quiver is full of them." There are certain Christian organizations whose websites proudly display pictures of their leaders with fifteen or more children and whose literature encourages fellow believers to do likewise.

Such a view is not representative of the general Christian view nationally, however, and is actually a rather small minority view among all the different denominations. Most churches feel that the original command to "be fruitful and multiply" has been fulfilled quite well with a present world population of around 7 billion people. Cultural differences need to be taken into account also; in an agrarian and pastoral setting thousands of years ago, children were a big asset; manual labor was needed and children were parents' "social security" in old age. Ancient Israel was always in danger from neighboring countries and thus children, especially males, were needed in the military; those personal quivers needed to be full. In modern America most people don't live on the farm, and raising children through college is an exceedingly expensive proposition; our military depends more on technology than many sons. Psalms 127:4-5 reflected a truth in ancient Israel's society that doesn't necessarily translate into our American cultural setting.

On the other side of the fence, however, the belief that our world is in serious trouble due to poverty stemming directly from human overpopulation is seriously suspect. Taiwan has a population that is around five times as dense as China's, and yet poverty is practically unknown in Taiwan. The Netherlands, believe it or not, has a population density four times that of China's. In terms of population density, Bermuda is more overpopulated than Bangladesh; Italy is denser than Pakistan; West Germany and India are practically tied. Sub-Sahara Africa, due to its large land mass, actually has a low population density – lower than that of the United States. The simple fact is that modern mechanized agricultural methods along with a supportive free economy model of government has done more to eliminate poverty in Western societies more than anything else. The United States has shipped millions of tons of wheat or corn to famine ravaged third world countries ruled by dictators or socialist/communist regimes only to watch much of that food rot on the docks due to political infighting and an inefficient distribution system.

There were dire predictions back in the 60's and 70's that the mushrooming world population would lead to mass famines even in modern developed nations if severe population control measures were not realized. Those assumptions have been proven to be wrong. There are now about 79 countries where the fertility rates have dropped below that famous statistical average of 2.1 children per family that is necessary simply to maintain a nation's current population. The fertility rates for Asia as a whole have fallen from 5.7 in the 60's to 2.8 presently; for Latin America it's 5.6 in the 60's to 2.7 today. Author Nicholas Eberstadt in *World Population Prospects for the Twenty-First Century: The Specter of 'Depopulation'?* printed in *"Earth Report 2000: Revisiting the True State of the Planet"* points out that "If present global demographic trends continue, the U.N. low-variant projections are likely. That would mean that world population would top out at 7.5 billion in 2040 and begin to decline."

The fears of the doom and gloom population out-of-control panicked folks on the political left in this country are simply contrary to facts. The "have all the kids that you possibly can because the Bible says so" philosophy of some leaders in Christianity is simply based on a misinterpretation of scripture due to not recognizing cultural differences. There has to be a balanced middle here somewhere, and we need to take a fresh look at this issue.

Note: Statistics were taken from "Environmental Stewardship" with several different contributing authors from the Jewish, Catholic, and Evangelical perspectives.[25]

THE DECLINE OF AMERICA?

The Tip of the Iceberg

Social conservatives are often caricatured as being obsessed with morals, to the exclusion of more pressing and important societal issues. They are often viewed as being more interested in what goes on in the privacy of people's homes, especially the bedrooms, than in addressing major economic problems. Concern over the gay-rights agenda takes precedence over unaffordable health insurance for many Americans; trying to limit abortion-on-demand supercedes trying to reduce the national debt; drawing attention to a 50% divorce rate trumps focusing on good-paying manufacturing jobs that are fleeing our shores for destitute foreigners willing to work for $2.00 an hour. As surely as there are many conservatives worried over jobs, health insurance, and the national debt, I'm equally convinced that this stereotype is not completely false. There is a grain of truth in every stereotype, or there would be no basis for the stereotype in the first place. Social conservatives can indeed obsess over carefully selected morals.

Obsessing only over bedroom issues is really indicative of a deeper, more disturbing reality, what I call the "tip of the iceberg" phenomenon. If there truly is a general moral decline going on in America over the last few decades, it would start showing itself in small subtle ways in those everyday interpersonal relations we have with each other, whether at home, at work, or in our government. It would affect our respect for each other and the public at large. It would start in the home, and an article buried back on page 9B in Sunday's *The Daily Herald* was extremely interesting in this regard. A study conducted by UCLA of modern families where both parents work outside the home reveals that many of these families are eroding from within, gradually losing intimacy, courteous verbal exchanges, spontaneous activities together, and a preoccupation with acquiring material possessions. Two of the basic factors at work here are increasing selfishness and greed, both moral qualities. It's really interesting that getting a divorce is considered more socially acceptable by many that the stigmatization of going for marital counseling. It's always easier to blame the other person.

Selfishness and greed have a way of working itself into every aspect of our social lives. Elected officials become enamored of their position and office, and gravitate towards the closed-door style of decision making circumventing the sunshine laws. Court dockets are stuffed with individuals suing anyone perceived to have deep pockets - insurance companies, automobile manufacturers, government, and last but not least fast food franchises. Malpractice suits have literally driven physicians out of certain areas of the United States or certain areas of medical practice. Whether it's too-hot coffee at McDonalds, or a relative who didn't make it through an operation, accidents are always someone's fault - someone with the money to pay us.

Corporate morals are often no better. Recent news articles revealed that certain Enron executives were laughing as the rolling power outages made life miserable for California residents. There never was an electrical shortage, only a shortage of morals and a surplus of greed. Much the same scenario was played out back in the 1980's with the "oil crisis." Drug manufacturers justify skyrocketing prescription drug costs as the price for future research, while grandma has to choose between her medicine and utility bill. Corporations can declare a financial emergency and dissolve employee pension plans, or simply move their jobs to India. We all applaud Martha Stewart for doing her time and returning to her company, but if insider trading and other irregularities continue to erode Americans' trust in the stock market, an actual crash is not an impossibility in the future. Basing the Social Security program on the stock market is basing it on peoples' morals.

At a more sickening level are the judges and politicians who are paid-off by the growing drug trade influence. Bribes have a way of perverting justice or even leading to the imprisonment of the innocent. Bribes have corrupted athletes and the outcome of some sporting events. Even lowly journalists are not immune. About a year ago a man by the name of Turki Al-Sudairi, the editor of the Saudi newspaper *Al-Riyadh,* revealed that the government of Saudia Arabia gives millions of dollars every year to bribe journalists around the world to slant articles towards being pro-Saudi and anti-Israel.

Just about every important societal issue can be analytically reduced to moral terms. Simple greed and selfishness ensnare famous TV evangelists and politicians alike. It's truly bipartisan and apolitical - Democrats, Republicans, liberals, and conservatives are all welcome in its suffocating embrace. When those conservatives harp on those "bedroom issues," just realize that they are focused only on the most obvious deviations from biblical standards that they see. Perhaps these issues are only a branch of the selfish moral monster iceberg that lies unseen beneath the waves. That's the one that can sink a nation, and the one that scripture has a lot to say about.

The Generational Slippery Slope

In discussing those hot-button social issues, I've noticed that people's perceptions often are couched in either/or terms - a pro or anti, black or white way of thinking. What's often not realized is that most social issues are part of a broad continuum with many stages in between opposites. As an example, consider the "number of sexual partners" arena. One can go from one-man one-woman traditional marriage to "committed but occasionally strays," to constant adultery, to serial monogamy "Hollywood style," to polygamy or polyandry, to casual "hooking-up" and group sex, and to prostitution. The degree of social disapproval on the average increases the further down the list you go.

Another example would be in the abortion debate arena. You can start with wanting children so badly as to adopt, to "letting nature take its course," to family planning through the rhythm method, to contraception, to the morning-after pill legal in other countries, to early-term abortion, late-term abortion, partial-birth abortion, to finally abandonment (the baby in the garbage dumpster syndrome) or infanticide (killing baby girls in China). It's a gradual shift from desperately wanting children to prevention to killing them.

A final example would be in the "sexual variety" category. You can start with heterosexuality, and then deviate into areas of homosexuality, bi-sexuality, incest, pedophilia, sadism/masochism, rape, to having sexual slaves. Again, public disapproval increases the further you go from the left to the right on these lists, with a few individuals quibbling over a particular item being a little further left or right on the list.

As a Christian conservative, I hold to the "left" positions in these lists as being the model that should be socially supported. I do so not only on a biblical basis, but also on a common sense basis. Many scientific studies have validated the nuclear family consisting of a mother and father as being the most supportive environment for children to be raised in, and the probability of sexually transmitted diseases increases with the number of partners, even with condom usage. Desiring a reasonable number of children is basic to the human condition, and without it we would quickly perish as a species.

As America moves more into a post-Christian society through increasing secularization, what young people think to be normal tends to be thought of in terms of what is legal. The government and the courts are being viewed as final arbiters in terms of what is right and wrong. The blue laws against infidelity were abandoned long ago, and last week there was a writer for USA Today arguing for the legalization of polygamy; the rationale was that the government should not be in our bedrooms. Once homosexuality is normalized fully by the law, the next step thirty years from now will be incest. I had a University of Michigan professor of Psychology play a cassette tape for our class of another professor arguing for the societal de-stigmatization of incest because it is statistically significant in every culture throughout the world.

The trend is becoming very evident - once a previously socially-disapproved of item on those lists becomes accepted as "normal," then a generation later the next item on the list becomes hotly debated, and the culture gradually slides down that slippery slope of desensitization to the abnormal. It's a trend that liberals often attempt to deny, but if we start looking past the length of our own lives we will recognize the shift. If your grandparents are still alive, talk to them about these issues, and from their recollections you can extrapolate into the future to see where we're headed.

It's No Myth

Back in my grandparent's day it was common practice here in the South to "seal the deal" on business transactions with a simple handshake. You didn't need a stack of signed legal paperwork and a bevy of lawyers – people simply took each other at their word. A lot of people left the doors to their house unlocked, or left the keys to their car in the ignition when at the convenience store. A cuss word uttered on the radio or television would have caused an immediate public outrage. Back in the 1950's it was scandalous to show two fully clothed adults in bed together. Divorce was not common and it was considered a real shame to be divorced. "Gangs" were to be found only in large cities like New York, Chicago, or Los Angeles.

A generation or two later and things are much different, except for a few folks who simply don't get it. The moral decline in our American culture is obvious to anyone 55 or older who still has a good memory. Back in those days it was a real embarrassment and public shame to be caught cheating. In the 1940's about 20% of college students admitted to cheating on tests in high school. Today somewhere between **75% and 98%** of college students admit to cheating in high school, depending on the survey used (from The Educational Testing Service Ad Council Campaign to Discourage Academic Cheating).

Back then if a young person stole something from a store and the parent found out about it, they were often severely disciplined and marched right back to the store for an apology session in front of the store manager. Today there are parents who actually look the other way when their kids use the "Five Finger Discount" method. Just in the last five years "more than 10 million people have been caught shoplifting" here in the U.S. and "more than $35 million dollars worth of goods" are shoplifted **each day** —information and statistics provided by the National Association for Shoplifting Prevention (NASP), a non-profit organization (www.shopliftingprevention.org).

Back then parents were expected to sacrifice for the sake of the kids and stay together through the good times and the bad times "till death do us part." The vast majority of children lived with both a mom and a dad. In the 30 year period between the early 1960's and the early 1990's, the divorce rate **quadrupled** and the percentage of children living in single-parent homes **tripled**. The illegitimate birth rate increased a whopping 419% with the teenage suicide rate going up 200%. Students' SAT scores dropped an average of 80 points during that same period. All this happened despite welfare spending increasing a whopping 630% and educational spending going up 225% – and yes, those percentages are inflation-adjusted (from the Index of Leading Cultural Indicators).

Street gangs were unheard of in the small towns of the South back then. By the 1970's less than half of the States, and less than 300 cities, reported problems with gang activity. By the late 1990's **all** the States and **over 2,500 cities** reported gang activity (from the U.S. Department of Justice – "The Growth of Youth Gang Problems in the U.S."). We have gang members living right here in Columbia.

Back then cheating on one's spouse was enough to get you financially "shook down" in divorce court; now it's the era of "No Fault" divorce. Sexual cheating is becoming more common with people under 30 years of age along with a trend of having multiple sexual partners before marriage (from "Young and Restless" – The Wall Street Journal, 11-28-2008). Professor of Sociology David Popenoe, PhD, at Rutgers University has stated that the biggest change in American society since the 1950's has been "less stable marriages and families." He notes juvenile delinquency has **increased 600%** over the past three decades – a natural consequence of divorce and absent fathers. A poll by the Wall Street Journal revealed that the majority of Americans believe "moral decline" is America's biggest problem.

Think of the categories of crime really coming to the fore in the last decade – Identity Theft, Road Rage, Phishing, Computer Viruses. Think of people looking for puddles to slip and fall in or "too hot" coffee to spill on themselves. Pyramid Schemes used to be something in the minds of High School cheerleaders. Almost all States in our Union now allow handgun permits – all due to the fear that people have of still living in Mayberry? From a time of it being a real shame to expose your "nakedness" to a time presently where the porn industry makes more money each year than all the pro football, baseball, and basketball franchises combined — that's $3,075 *every second* with 28,258 internet users *every second* (from FamilySafeMedia.com).

Still there are some folks who just don't get it. They are usually too young to remember the change over the decades; they haven't asked their grandparents what it was like back then; or they are simply repeating tired old liberal talking points about the myth of moral decline that the conservatives are supposedly foisting on the public. Lack of historical communal memory is a shameful thing.

THE BIBLE IS SIMPLE
SO WHY SEMINARIES?

Intellectual Curiosity

I was the kid who always asked those embarrassing questions to my teachers – not intentionally embarrassing, but merely because of my penchant for trying to make sense of things even if it meant calling into question the validity of what I had been taught. That type of natural intellectual curiosity is lauded in the university, patiently tolerated in high school, but absolutely abhorred in the church I attended all through my youth. Church is the one place where often you are expected to accept everything taught unquestioningly – otherwise you are harboring doubt or, worse yet, trying to be a troublemaker. Intellectual curiosity is often not a prized commodity in fundamentalist churches nearly as much as being quiet, sitting still, memorizing verses, and never making waves.

I still feel a bit sorry for my young adult Sunday School teacher Mrs. Russell. She was busy one Sunday morning explaining to us how awe-inspiring angels are flying from heaven down here to earth with their powerful wings when I could no longer resist the urge to pop-off with "Wait a minute, wings don't work in the vacuum of space"! She turned a little red and floundered for words in trying to come up with an explanation that never really did resolve anything.

Then there was the day I asked my pastor, Rev. Mossman, why the Bible never mentioned the dinosaurs and also how there could be "day 1, day 2, and day 3" when the sun and moon were not created until "day 4." He thought about that for a few weeks and finally told me he had no idea why. He also seemed to avoid me somewhat after that.

Then there was the story about the Tower of Babel – where the people were trying to build a tower that "reached into the heavens." Preachers would assert that God was so concerned that the people might actually accomplish this task and invade God's personal home that He confused their languages to prevent it. I remember thinking incredulously "Have they really thought seriously about what they are saying? What would ancient peoples do when they reached an elevation depleted of oxygen? Does God's heaven exist floating in the clouds somewhere? What if heaven is located billions of light-years out there in the universe somewhere?" A good analogy would be ants crawling on a beach ball trying to construct an anthill one inch high in hopes of reaching the moon – all while the beach ball is spinning in the air.

It's not that I'm trying to write a damning indictment of all fundamentalist churches such as the one I was raised in – I actually appreciate their fidelity to the inspiration of scripture and the necessity of spiritual salvation. It's simply that "no embarrassing questions allowed" mindset that is so stultifying to a youngster's intellectual development that I find counterproductive – and a reason why we lose so many of our young people once they go off to college. My faith has been strengthened, not weakened, in the quest for answers to questions like these and many more.

Many years later I discovered that there are reasonable explanations for those questions that are congruent with sound thinking. Angels generally do not have wings (except for a certain type that stay permanently in heaven); that heaven could possibly be located in a parallel dimension right next door to us (which would explain how Jesus and angels could "appear" and "disappear" at will); that the seven days of creation could be in symbolical form; that dinosaurs fit perfectly well into the Gap theory, progressive creationism, and theistic evolution (although the latter does not fit well with Genesis); and that the Tower of Babel was built for an entirely different reason than what was preached. Archaeologists have uncovered Babylonian ziggurats that had seven terraces in honor of the seven "planetary deities" with the signs of the zodiac being inscribed around the top. The towers were thought to be approaches to heaven and the spirit world beyond – and that the stars had a divine influence on peoples' lives – just like in astrology today. The Tower of Babel is thought to be an early prototype of these ziggurats, and God was concerned that people actually thought they could gain entrance to the "Great Beyond" depending on the stars for guidance in a false religious system rather than on the true God himself. That makes a whole lot more sense as the Old Testament is chock-full of narratives wherein God is moved to anger by people trying to invent their own religion or serve false idol gods.

Going through Bible college, I discovered whole books that were written answering questions such as these by authors who were devout Christians as well as academically brilliant. It is critically important not to quash an inquisitive young mind with a thunderous "Because I —the Bible says so" roar of indignant anger. Human reasoning is not automatically condemned by God – God himself says in Isaiah 1:18 "Come now, let us reason together says the Lord…" It's entirely reasonable, and "Christianly," to be reasonably questioning.

Pursuing that Master's Degree

It seems like an eternity ago that I started this long journey towards achieving a Master's Degree in Biblical Literature – the year 2000 to be precise. There were a few undergraduate classes I had to take first (I had a Bachelor of Science from the University of Michigan previously), then a 5 year program of classes, then a 2 year thesis project, then a change of major and two more classes. All my classes are now completed; my last project is now a "Capstone Paper" in which I formulate my own philosophy of ministry from concepts learned through all my prior classes. By the end of this coming January all the requirements will be met and I will finally have that "sheepskin" hanging on the wall of my study den.

The end result of all this study is the realization that I am honestly not a scholar. I've come to that conclusion carrying a 4.0 GPA all through my program. A true scholar is not someone who merely has read a ton of scholarly books; a scholar is one who makes their living working in the academic world authoring books or articles in scholarly publications, doing research into uninvestigated areas, teaching at universities or seminaries, becoming proficient in ancient Biblical languages and working in translation efforts and et cetera. Most likely I would need a little higher IQ level and be about 30 years younger to have a realistic chance of working in that sphere of human endeavor. I have merely been a very good student with a knack for comprehending sometimes rather abstruse academic debates and theological promulgations and filling up a 5 gallon bucket full of academic writing assignments analyzing them.

I started this journey probably just like a lot of students in religious studies – thinking that my own church denomination had a corner on most Biblical truth and I was merely honing my skills to verify the veracity of that assumption – and to become a better researcher, public speaker, and writer along the way. My upbringing was Pentecostal and so was the university I had chosen. Global University is affiliated with the Assemblies of God denomination. Now that I am very close to graduating with a Master's degree from a Pentecostal college, I realize I am no longer Pentecostal. Pentecostals believe that every Christian should "speak in tongues" (languages not learned) — not that all Christians do or even that all members of Pentecostal churches do, but rather that the opportunity is there and should be sought by all Christians. Basically that is a violation of one of the hermeneutical rules in one of my classes — if Jesus or the Apostles had stated that all Christians for all times should "speak in tongues" then that would have settled the matter. They didn't – the assumption is made because in 3 of 5 recorded instances in the Book of Acts of baptism in the Holy Spirit, they spoke in tongues; the other two incidents are left unspecified. Also the Apostle Paul taught that spiritual gifts are given to certain members of Christ's body, the church, as God so wills, and the answer to Paul's rhetorical question of "Do all speak in tongues?" (1 Corinthians 12:30) is a resounding "NO" – which my church always conveniently ignored. Technically I am no longer a classical Pentecostal.

I do believe that God does bless some Christians with such supernatural gifts, so that pretty much leaves me out of most Baptist, Methodist, and Lutheran churches. Seeing no Biblical contradiction with having musical instruments in church worship services leaves me out of the Churches of Christ. I prefer the congregational model of church government a bit more than the centralized hierarchical top-down model, so that leaves out the "high churches," such as Presbyterian and Episcopal. I fully empathize with the Reformer's "Sola Scriptura" principle that the Scripture has authority over the church and not vice versa, so that leaves me out of Roman Catholicism. At this point I honestly don't think I line-up fully with any denomination's creedal formulations. I guess I'm simply a Christian.

One thing I treasure about this educational journey is the variety of views I was allowed to enjoy – authors of my textbooks have come from the Baptist, Pentecostal, Lutheran, Methodist, Presbyterian, Vineyard, Roman Catholic, Swedish Evangelical Free Church, and nondenominational churches. There was even one Mormon, Stephen Covey with his *Seven Habits of Highly Successful People*, even though Mormonism isn't strictly "Christian" because of their belief in the Book of Mormon. That variety broadened my view and enlarged my horizons – which allowed me to realize that there are a lot of good Christians in a variety of church denominations, many of whom are quite scholarly. In our basic beliefs of faith we have more in common than our differences in practice. It's been worth twelve years of losing my weekends holed up in my study den just to realize that.

Advanced Biblical Studies Foster Humility

I don't write quite as many editorial articles as I used to and the reason can be summed up in one word —thesis. It's been a long arduous journey over the last seven years working on this graduate degree one class at a time while working full-time in a manufacturing environment, so the final phase is a welcome sight to me. It's also a daunting task, unlike anything I've ever encountered.

A sense of humility is probably the most beneficial self-improvement I've noticed through these studies. I tended to be somewhat of an iconoclastic, self-taught Biblical student who had an inflated sense of my intellectual prowess before I began. I had studied the Bible through several times along with several good Christian books and commentaries and thought "How much more could there be to learn about one book?"

The blatant naiveté in retrospect is truly embarrassing. For those of you with a similar viewpoint, I issue a challenge: go to any of several good theological libraries in the Nashville area. Walk past aisle after aisle of scholarly tomes stacked seven high in rows, pull one out at random now and then, and read a few pages in it. You will, in short order, come to appreciate both the depth and breadth of scholarly learning on a myriad of topics all related to Christianity or the Bible. If I someday complete a PhD, then I will have read much less than 1 percent of all theological books ever written. It's all about what you specialize in, and hopefully contribute something original to, in your field of endeavor.

Sometimes people in town here mistakenly think I'm a scholar or worse yet, as one fellow put it "Oh, I recognize you — you're that town theologian and editorial writer!" I then have to patiently explain that I have no right to such an illustrious title. Scholars live their lives usually in a university setting teaching classes and writing books or professional journal articles. Theologians usually serve within church denominations' seminaries doing the same. If you are not teaching classes or haven't been published, then you really aren't one.

A thesis requires you to pose a question that needs an answer — the answer to which will yield something somewhat original in your field of study. It can be a slightly different interpretation of a well-known concept that needs corroborating evidence; comparing and contrasting two different points of view from a different angle than looked at before in the scholarly world; investigating fresh archaeological evidence that sheds new light on a particular period of church history, etc. The necessary component is the originality.

Before you can even start on your own idea you have to search through previous generation's research related to your topic — including books, periodicals, and even others' Master's or PhD dissertations to be sure you aren't replicating someone else's work. You often find that you are not the first. Once you do have something truly original, you have to search bibliographies to find everything related to your topic. Each scholarly book you read will have a bibliography at the end listing all the books that author relied on in his or her research. You then have to find and read all those books that are relevant and repeat the process with the bibliographies at the ends of those books. It's exhausting and seemingly endless.

Your preliminary thesis then gets batted around between members of an academic committee chosen just for you. They will find errors or points of weakness and suggest more books to help you remedy your deficiencies. Constant rejections and revisions are the norm. The process does tend to engender humility.

On any given day that I have free time, you might find me searching through Global's online theological library or in the basement of Vanderbilt's library (Why are the theological libraries usually in the basement of universities? I call it the dungeon with plumbing pipes running overhead everywhere.) Sometimes I'm in Belmont's or Lipscomb's theological library. The thought struck me recently that I was sitting there in a Church-of-Christ supported institution reading a book by a German author from a Presbyterian perspective while comparing it to my own Pentecostal background. I do enjoy the cross-denominational aspect of my studies.

For those of you curious about the thesis process, that's it in a highly compressed nutshell. I'm hoping to replace the time I used to have perusing news sources for editorial articles with interesting interdenominational nuggets of Biblical research now and then. Just don't call me a scholar or a theologian; I'm far from that. Right now I'm just a good student and a bookworm.

Holier Than Thou?
Not a Bible Scholar...

It arrived in the mail last Saturday in a rather nondescript plain manila envelope; inside was my diploma from Global University located in Springfield, Missouri. There was the customary heavy textured certificate embossed with the flashy gold seal bearing the proclamation "In recognition of the successful fulfillment of the program requirements; Stephen Rowland is awarded the degree of Master of Arts in Biblical Studies..." Enclosed was an invitation to membership to the Delta Epsilon Tau International Honor Society for high grades in distance learning institutions.

My wife and family members congratulated me, but honestly this achievement has been bittersweet. The first attitude that I often encountered from church folks was that of bewilderment or puzzlement – why did I think it necessary to pursue a Master's degree in the Bible? Most pastors in my denomination didn't have a formal degree and they were successful, so why the effort? Their view was that the Bible is simple – anyone can read and understand it. Isn't a formal degree just complicating the obvious? Of course they had never picked up a theology book to read, so they were basing their view on something with which they had no knowledge or experience. Neither had they ever attended a church where the pastor had graduated from a seminary so that they could hear the difference. Apparently they had never considered the hundreds of different denominations here in the U.S., all of which believe somewhat differently when it comes to doctrine. If the Bible is exceedingly simple with nothing left to interpretation then everyone would believe exactly the same way.

The second attitude was several misunderstandings about what a formal education in the Bible consisted of – some thought I was supposed to be a "walking Biblical encyclopedia" spouting off Biblical facts and trivia at one's request. Others thought I should be able to preach a whole sermon based on the definition of a single Biblical word parsing out the fine shades of meaning from the original Hebrew or Greek. Others wanted to play that game of "Gotcha" – they would test me on some obscure Biblical trivia fact, and if I could not recall the answer, they would then smugly tell me the answer and leave with that "So if that's what a Bible college program produces, it's not worth much!" attitude. One fellow suggested that if I was not majoring in Hebrew or Greek to aid in translation efforts, then my college was probably a diploma mill!

Some folks have the idea that studying Bible doctrine is somehow contrary to encouraging ecumenical efforts – promoting friendly relations between denominations. Apparently we should keep everything very simple to prevent arguing and bad feelings. Others think that if spiritual truth is to be found, it must be simple to be true. Of course we don't have that "truth conception" about other professions – law, engineering, science, surgery, etc.

One local pastor informed me that seminary professors were former unsuccessful pastors who went off to college, got educated, returned to pastor churches of 20 or 30 members, then wanted to tell everyone else how to pastor! That was the biggest slam, and a completely skewed caricature of Bible professors I had ever heard. That assessment would surely have been news to some of my professor mentors who pastored very large churches. It also ignored the fact that quite a few pastors of large churches take correspondence Bible courses along the way to help them improve in Biblical exegesis.

The point is this: if you decide to go off to seminary, or take correspondence Bible courses, don't expect everyone to pat you on the back. If higher education is not the norm in your denomination, or if your pastor is uneducated, then there will be an intrinsic unstated suspicion of you. Human nature is to be suspicious or fearful of what we do not know, and if our ego is fragile, to view any church member going down the Bible college road as possible "unwelcome competition." People might think they are "smart" and they could possibly cause a schism.

Once you enter a world full of other pastors' and Christian scholars' writings and preachings outside of your own church, you have to lay at the altar of personal self-sacrifice that enlarged ego. Sometimes other scholars see the Bible differently than you, and sometimes they are right. Once you embark on that journey, however, the biggest pat on the back you can get is from the One you serve on High. He will reward your diligent efforts, and you won't have to worry about His ego.

Footnotes

1. http://www.bibleliteracy.org/site/PressRoom/press_execsum.htm

2. http://www.christianitytoday.com/ct/2006/juneweb-only/126-41.0.html

3. Ledewitz, Bruce. 2007. *American Religious Democracy: Coming to Terms with the End of Secular Politics.* Praeger Publishing.

4. http://70.32.78.39/content/banker-poor?page=1

5. http://www.fondationchirac.eu/en/innovative-financements-for-development/

6. http://www.american.com/archive/2007/november-december-magazine-contents/what-makes-a-terrorist

7. http://www.memri.org/report/en/0/0/0/0/0/0/1304.htm

8. http://www.letusreason.org/islam12.htm

9. http://catholicexchange.com/comparing-god-and-allah---fundamental-considerations/ Also Quran 4:65

10. http://www.meforum.org/2538/taqiyya-islam-rules-of-war

11. http://www.the-new-way.org/testimonies/conv_varie_049_the_power_of_prayer.html

12. http://www.afajournal.org/2005/january/1.05Hardwired.asp

13. http://en.wikipedia.org/wiki/Stanford_prison_experiment

14. http://en.wikipedia.org/wiki/Milgram_experiment

15. Pearcy, Nancy R. and Charles B. Thaxton. 1994. *The Soul of Science: Christian Faith and Natural Philosophy*. (page 38). Crossway Books: Wheaton, Illinois

16. Johnson, Phillip E. 1993. *Darwin on Trial*. (page 37). InterVarsity Press: Downers Grove, IL

17. Ibid, pp 40

18. Ibid, pp 50

19. Morris, Henry. 1974. *Scientific Creationism*. Creation-Life Publishers: San Diego, California

20. Van Till, Howard J. with Davis A. Young and Clarence Menninga. 1988. *Science Held Hostage*. InterVarsity Press: Downers Grove, Illinois

21. Berry, R.J. 1996. in *Time Magazine* (Oct 28).

22. Ross, Hugh. 1991. *The Fingerprint of God*. Page 132. Promise Publishing Co: Orange, CA

23. http://www.familywatchinternational.org/fwi/why_marriage.cfm

24. Stanton, Glenn T. 1997. *Why Marriage Matters: Reasons to Believe in Marriage in Postmodern Society.* NavPress: Colorado Springs, CO

25. Berry, R.J. Sam. 2006. *Environmental Stewardship: Critical Perspective – Past and Present.* T&T Clark International

About the Author

Stephen has a Bachelor of Science degree from the University of Michigan and a Master of Arts in Biblical Literature from Global University. He has been an editorialist for **The Daily Herald** in Columbia, Tennessee for eight years and was the graduate "Reflections Speaker" at Commencement ceremonies for Global University in June of 2012. He served as chaplain for the Knights for Christ, the Columbia chapter of the Christian Motorcyclists Association, from 2010 to 2011. Stephen works for General Motors in Spring Hill, Tennessee and is married to Susan; they happily reside in Columbia, Tennessee.

CPSIA information can be obtained at www.ICGtesting.com
Printed in the USA
LVOW121234240912

300063LV00002B/1/P

9 781462 720460